About the Author

Jillian Venters, "The Lady of the Manners," was a fairly spooky and morbid child. When she discovered the existence of the Gothic sub culture, she clapped her hands with glee and fell upon it like a babybat upon a box of Count Chocula cereal. Since then, the Lady of the Manners has spent a not inconsiderable amount of time trying to gently persuade others in her chosen subculture that being a Goth and being polite is much, much more subversive than just wearing black T-shirts with "edgy" sayings on them.

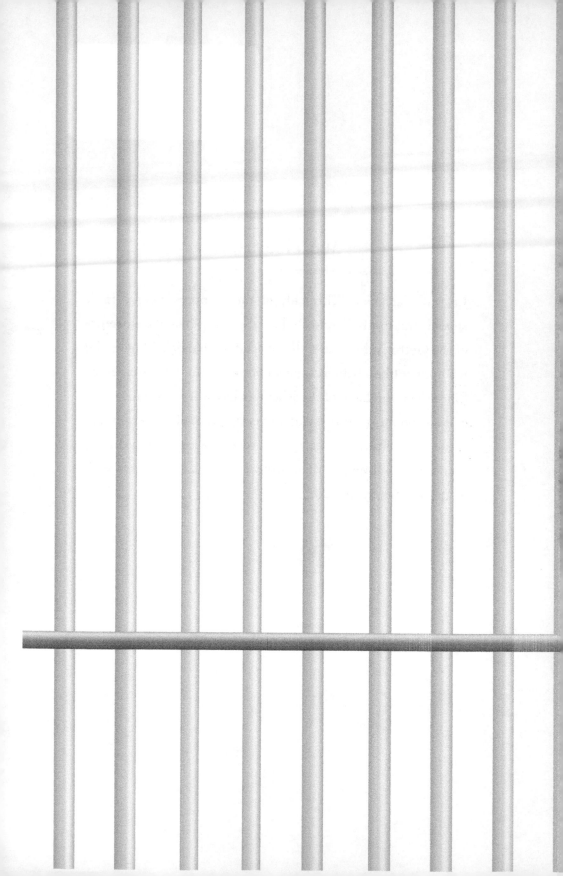

Gothic
Charm School

Gothic Charm School

An Essential Guide for Goths and Those Who Love Them

Jillian Venters

with Illustrations by Pete Venters

HARPER

NEW YORK · LONDON · TORONTO · SYDNEY

HARPER

HarperCollins books may be purchased for educational, business, or sales promotional use. For information please write: Special Markets Department, HarperCollins Publishers, 10 East 53rd Street, New York, NY 10022.

FIRST EDITION

Designed by Aline C. Pace

Library of Congress Cataloging-in-Publication Data is available upon request.

ISBN 978-0-06-166916-3

HB 06.07.2023

For all the past and present readers of
Gothic Charm School.
For Mom and Dad, for always encouraging
me to be whomever I wanted.
For Pete, for love, support, and sanity checks.
And for Clovis. He knows why.

Acknowledgments

An enormous bouquet of black and pink roses and sparkly bats
are owed with gratitude to the following people:

Lauren Abramo, Acid PopTart, Allyson Beatrice, BlueJay,
Doug Carter, Jennifer Luckman Carter, Drew Dalzel, Donna Davies,
Sarah Durand, Juliana Egley, Lisa Van Every, Barbara Caridad Ferrer,
Neil Gaiman, Amy Garvey, Brittany Hamblin, Kij Johnson, Kambriel,
Evelyn Kriete, Emily Krump, Beverly Leoczko, Jennifer Lovely,
Thea Maia, Marc17, Darren McKeeman,
Lillian "Princess Tickybox" Marcontell, Pleiades McRae Marcontell,
Lisa Mesplay, Katie Mineke, Monsignor, Lee Neugebauer,
Elena Okrent, Heather Pate, Queenie, Alexia Roy, David Smay, Stax,
Kristin Taylor, S.A. Throop, Alex von Hochtritt, and the various
and sundry creatures of the night in the Gothic world that have
written to me throughout the years.

Contents

 An Introduction   **1**

- Or why Goths *must* cultivate better manners than other people, and just who is this Lady of the Manners chick, anyway?

 Chapter 1: Am I a Goth?   **7**

- A very brief recitation of the history of the Goth subculture
- Some signs and symptoms of having a gothy mindset
- The difference between being a Goth, a NotAGoth, and not being a Goth yourself but being Goth-friendly
- The age gap (also known as, "Am I too old for this?")
- Do you have to be spooky every day?
- Why you shouldn't believe everything you read on the Internet, including those silly quizzes

 Chapter 2: I'm Not a Goth, But I Have Some Questions About Them . . .   **31**

- Common misconceptions about Goths
- Can I comment on their clothing or makeup and ask if they make their own clothes?

- A brief primer on how to behave and what to wear if you decide to explore the Goth scene with your spooky acquaintances
- If a Goth is inexplicably mean to me in the Hot Topic where I get my hair dye, can I name-check you and threaten to file a report? (Oh, how the Lady of the Manners wishes that would work!)

 Chapter 3: Babygoths   **57**

- How to show support to your babygoth or babybat without relinquishing the keys to the hearse, and everything you need to know to Not Freak Out
- What if my children hide behind me wide-eyed?
- What if my children run toward them shrieking with glee?
- How do I explain Goth to my children if they ask me about it?
- Goth parents and raising the next generation of babybats

 Chapter 4: Help! I'm a Goth and My Parent/ Friend/Significant Other/Coworker Doesn't Understand Me!   **75**

- How to reassure people you aren't a Satanist, drug fiend, or psycho killer
- Helpful tips for convincing your parents to let you express your-self through your clothing (but don't kid yourself: the Lady of the Manners wouldn't let you wear a corset to school either)
- Goths and school (and why these aren't necessarily the best years of your life)
- Dealing with roommates

 Chapter 5: Gothy Clichés and Why They're So Pervasive   **93**

- Why friends don't let friends dress like the Crow
- No, we don't all think we're vampires (but we *do* read a lot of vampire books)

- No, you don't have to be depressed to be a Goth
- So you say you're not a Goth, but people keep assuming you are
- The roots of Goth's dark garden
- Why being called a cliché isn't such a bad thing

Chapter 6: Goths and Romance   115

- Etiquette for and about crushes
- Flirting and dating
- "But why are you with *him/her?!*"
- Goths and Valentine's Day
- Breakups, heartbreak, and mobbing the newly single
- Goth weddings (both weddings for Goths and Goths attending "normal" weddings)

Chapter 7: Socializing, Cliques, and Gossip   145

- Why being polite to people you don't like is important
- Why being circumspect about gossip and catty commentary is even *more* important
- The difference between snarkiness and cattiness
- The difference between self-confidence and self-absorption
- The difference between exclusivity and snobbishness
- Subcultural crossovers and the blurring of boundaries
- The Internet is not Real Life (with an aside about the Great Flounce-Off)
- Why polite honesty doesn't always have the hoped-for effect

**Chapter 8: Fashion: One of the
Great Goth Obsessions   169**

- The never-ending debate about fashion vs. music (part 1)
- Appropriate attire suggestions for job interviews, the corporate world, family get-togethers, the summer heat, the chill of winter, and other events

- Dress codes (both spoken and unspoken)
- What to do when people ask you why you're dressed like that
- What to do when Goth becomes the darling of the fashion industry
- The basics of assembling a gothy wardrobe
- Why no one really has an "original" Goth Look, so get over yourselves already

Chapter 9: Dance the Ghost with Me: Music and Gothy Club and Concert Etiquette   203

- The never-ending debate about music vs. fashion (part 2)
- Why the ElderGoths are always so cranky about the mainstream eyeliner-wearing band du jour
- Why Marilyn Manson is not a Goth
- Manners on the dance floor
- Manners and socializing at the club (including "don't touch people without invitation" and "always be nice to the staff")
- Why yelling "Freebird!" isn't as amusing as you might think and other advice for concertgoers
- A special section about dealing with or being a tourist at a Goth club or event

Chapter 10: Where Do We Go from Here?   227

- The possible future of Goth and the Lady of the Manners's hopes for it (plus a couple of her fears, though she's sure they won't come to pass)

Gothic
Charm School

An Introduction

Or why Goths *must* cultivate better manners than other people, and just who is this Lady of the Manners chick, anyway?

The Lady of the Manners has heard this complaint time and time again from her fellow Goths: "Why should I put so much effort into being polite to people who aren't going to be considerate to me?" The Lady of the Manners certainly understands the complaint, because it can be very disheartening and dispiriting (and other dismal-sounding words) to be as polite toward strangers as possible and have those strangers respond not in kind, but with rudeness, boorish behavior, and even sometimes with threats and violence. Wouldn't it be better if we gloomily romantic and darkly garbed folk all adopted a shield of preemptive scorn and hostility?

No. No, it wouldn't be better. Because those rude and boorish strangers would take our scorn and hostility as an open invitation to behave in even worse ways toward us than they do now. Because such behavior would feed the suspicion and fear with which many people regard Goths. Because more parents would regard their fledgling Goth children with extra worry and concern. Because even more people would be skeptical about whether Goths can be good employees or people to be trusted.

Yes, the Lady of the Manners is well aware that all sorts of people are openly rude and hostile to everyone they meet, and they seem to do just fine. But the Lady of the Manners really does believe that no matter how well those sorts of people seem to be doing, they probably would do even better if they weren't, well, jerks. Polite kindness isn't weakness, no matter what some people think.

There's an added benefit to being a Goth and having good manners: it's actually more shocking to some people than the "Booooo! I'm so spooky and scary!" freak show antics they expect from Goths. Looking like you've just come from a gathering with a particularly sinister dress code *and* being gracious and polite messes with some people's heads far more effectively than anything else you might be able to think up.

Does this mean that when people yell, "Nice costume!" or, "Halloween is over, freak!" at you, you should quash your annoyance and ignore them? Sometimes, yes, you should. But sometimes you could smile widely and, in your friendliest and politest tone, respond with, "Oh, I dress this way all the time! What are *you* in costume as?" or, "It isn't Halloween? Oh, I must have forgotten to change the calendar!" or, "Oh my God! I was wearing jeans and a T-shirt when I left the house! What happened to me?!" The Lady of the Manners has occasionally indulged herself in such responses, not that they made a bit of difference to the cretin who started the confrontation. You see, Snarklings, there are many times when trying to change people's perceptions isn't worth the effort. The best way to make your displeasure clear is to simply ignore them. Offer a quick icy glance, and then act as if the rude person doesn't exist.

(Mind you, if it looks like the situation is going to escalate into an attack, *do not* ignore the taunts. Instead, get away as quickly as possible and call the police. The Lady of the Manners does not want anyone to be injured in the name of being polite, and she is sadly aware that some people do react with violence to things they don't like or understand.)

The Lady of the Manners isn't asking you to hold hands and have a joyful sing-along with everyone you meet. Nor is she asking you to be outgoing and friendly toward every person who ever asks you questions about your gothy tendencies. The Lady of the Manners *is* asking that you don't automatically glower, snarl, or retreat behind a wall of sarcastic commentary. That's all. Really, it's a pretty simple idea.

So who is this Lady of the Manners person, and why is she lecturing and haranguing . . . er, offering gothy and non-gothy people advice? Here, let the Lady of the Manners dispense with the third-person frivolity and affectation for a few paragraphs and introduce herself.

Hi, I'm Jillian. I've been drawn to the gloom-shrouded and spooky side of life for as long as I can remember. Am I claiming to always have been a Goth? No, not at all. But I've always been interested in dark, opulent clothing, in otherworldly stories, in the supernatural and terror, and in looking at the world around me in a different way. I just didn't know there was a subculture that embraced and enveloped all those things (and more) until my early twenties. When I discovered that there were other people like me, that there was a whole movement I could gleefully plunder for more interests, activities, and socializing, I joyfully joined the darkling throng and haven't looked back.

Well, perhaps "joyfully" isn't quite the right word. You see, while I did meet other black-clad eccentrics who accepted me, I also ran into a lot of people who were . . . less than friendly. Impolite, you might say. Some were other Goths, who were seemingly determined to be surly toward everyone while simultaneously carrying a coffin-sized chip on their shoulders about the non-Goth jerks who treated them badly. They somehow felt that they were going to be sneered at or regarded with fear and loathing, and that armoring themselves with a thick coating of sarcasm, resentment, and disdainful looks was the only way to go. Other impolite souls were non-Goths who were everything the surly and rude Goths feared. They were the ones making sarcastic comments meant to be overheard, jeering at me and my spooky friends. They were the people who drew back from us in fear because they just knew that Goths were all creepy freaks who were going to attack them or cast evil spells on them. They were the people who assumed we were going to be rude and unkind to them—all of these assumptions because my friends and I chose to express ourselves through our appearance and to talk openly about the things that interested us.

The rudeness and bad behavior on both sides of the shadowy divide bugged me. I was raised to believe that you should treat people the way you wanted to be treated, and that the way a person looks shouldn't matter. In addition to those beliefs, I somehow ended up being one of those people others turn to for advice. Then, one fateful day, an acquaintance who was putting together a Goth webzine mentioned that he wanted to include some nonfiction content, and asked me if there was anything I might want to contribute. I thought about it and said, "Ooh, how about a gothy advice column? Good manners for Goths, why you shouldn't dress like the Crow, or how, if you're going to wear whiteface, you should make sure you apply it on your damn ears and neck—stuff like that?" My friend thought my idea sounded great, and thus I found myself giving my e-mail address and advice to complete strangers.

That was over a decade ago. As the years have passed, I've found myself addressing certain topics over and over: reassuring parents that having a child with gothy tendencies isn't a bad thing, giving advice to other Goths about how to deal with parents or coworkers who are unsure about how to act around darkly dressed creatures, how to deal with the slings and arrows that constantly seem to be flung at Goths, all while watching the Goth subculture creep out from the shadows and attract more attention from the mainstream media and "normal" folks. And the more prominent and well-recognized Goth becomes, the bigger the chances that misunderstandings and just flat-out *wrong* information will be taken as the absolute gospel truth about our subculture.

Which is why I try to be a good example and show Goths and non-Goths that it is possible to be a black-clad eccentric *and* a good person, that just because someone is interested in a dark, spooky, and more somber definition of beauty doesn't mean that he or she should be viewed with fear and suspicion. It's my hope that this book will be informative and entertaining, and that it will help Goths be better understood. And with that, it's time for me to pin my hat back on and slip back into the Lady of the Manners's third-person mannerisms.

Won't you please turn the page and join me in this shadowy, mysterious, charming world that I call home?

ONE

Am I a Goth?

A very brief recitation of the history of the Goth subculture

So where does this Goth (or Gothic) thing come from? While it would be tedious to detail the Complete History of Goth, context is always useful.

The Goth subculture as it is known today began as an offshoot of punk rock that mixed a flair for the theatrical and a fondness of campy horror movies. While every cultural movement or phase has cast its own dark shadows (vampy flappers and sinister rakes, noir femmes fatales, black-clad occult types reading tarot cards by candlelight), those shadows never really seemed to flow together into a glorious tapestry of velvet-edged darkness in the U.K. and U.S. until the late '70s and early '80s.

Goth draws from such varied sources as architecture (yes, those lovely cathedrals and castles in glorious ruin), with the Romantic movement of the late eighteenth and early nineteenth centuries prompting the well-to-do to renovate their homes to imitate medieval castles or abbeys. Gothic novels lurched out of the darkness with *The Castle of Otranto* by Horace Walpole, *The Monk* by Matthew Gregory Lewis, the works of Ann Radcliffe (one of the bestselling authors of the late eighteenth century), and Mary Shelley's *Frankenstein*. The restless spirits they summoned have cast shadows over fiction ever since. *Wuthering Heights*, *Dracula*, the works of Edgar Allan Poe, and swarms of romance novels all feature Gothic themes, even if some readers don't immediately recognize them as Gothic. The feelings of gloom, suspense, and dread—the long and skittering fingers of Gothic fiction—allow people to vicariously experience the thrills and chills of the otherworldly and supernatural without fearing for their safety or sanity. Victorian spiritualism and occultism, gathering around a candlelit table and trying to contact dead loved ones, was all the rage at the best parties of the era, adding another layer to the history of Goth, while the Victorians' elaborate mourning clothing and customs have provided Goths with not only clothing styles to mimic, but also a host of charmingly eccentric behaviors and mannerisms to adopt. (What, you mean not everyone has a collection of handkerchiefs edged in black lace?)

What's that, you say? You didn't realize that Goth had such a long history? Oh yes, Goth is not just some flash-in-the-pan teen fad. Why, this current incarnation of the Goth subculture has been gliding around elegantly for almost thirty years now. And that's just musically speaking. Television series such as *The Addams Family*, *The Munsters*, and *Dark Shadows* all provided a flickering family tree in black and white images and a strong pop culture foundation for the spookily inclined. Even key modern Goth touchstones such as *Beetlejuice* and *The Nightmare Before Christmas* are over fifteen years old. In fact, in the case of *The Nightmare Before Christmas*, more tie-in merchandise has been manufactured in the past few years than was available when the movie was released in 1993. (The Lady of the Manners, while a bit cynically amused at the proliferation of Jack Skellington's face, is quite pleased with her *Nightmare Before Christmas*–decorated bathroom, thankyouverymuch.)

Facts such as these make Goths of the Lady of the Manners's generation feel just a touch culture-lagged and often leave us muttering phrases like, "Back in my day, we had to mail order music from obscure little catalogs! We had to make our own fishnet shirts out of old tights! We had to dye our hair with Kool-Aid! We had to burn sticks to make our own eyeliner! Now anyone can go to the mall and buy a complete off-the-rack Goth outfit! You kids get offa my lawn . . ."

Oh, fine. We didn't really have to burn sticks to make our own eyeliner. But yes, we did make our own fishnet shirts out of old tights, and if you saw another person clad in all black with elaborate hair and makeup, you both did the mutual freak nod of recognition. You might not have known this person, but you could assume he or she was probably a spooky type interested in some of the same things that you were.

The current dark flowering of Goth is generally considered to have started when Bauhaus released "Bela Lugosi's Dead" in 1979. Yes, Joy Division and Siouxsie and the Banshees had already released albums, and there were all sorts of pale creatures in black lurking around the punk scene, but Peter Murphy crooning about red velvet lining a black box and virginal brides filing past his tomb gave those same creatures something to *really* focus their attention on. In 1982, the Batcave opened in London, giving the self-styled creatures of the night a place to be and be seen. The Batcave attracted a fair amount of attention from the media, spreading the seeds of the Goth subculture across the U.K. At the same time in the U.S., the deathrock scene was clawing its way out of the graveyard with its own horror-laced take on punk.

All of these elements grew and mutated, appropriating symbols from Gothic literature, horror movies, Victorian fashions, and anything from any historical era that had earned the label "decadent." Nowadays there are so many different splinter factions crowded under the Goth label (as if it were a giant parasol, shielding everyone from the harsh and frightening sun) that not only are there inter-subculture squabbles about what is and isn't *really* part of Goth, but there are huge lists and Internet quizzes to help people try to figure out what type of Goth they might be. Romantigoths, punkgoths, mopeygoths, perkygoths—all of these and more are labels the Lady of the Manners has seen tossed around, along with less-flattering terms such as mallgoth or spookykid, usually aimed at the youngsters who inadvertently help encourage that "Goth is just a teen phase" misconception.

Some signs and symptoms of having a gothy mindset

When someone says "Goth," certain images or interests come to mind. A not-in-any-way-complete list of them, in no particular order:

 Black clothing, of course; perhaps with a vaguely Victorian or otherwise antique air to it

 A somewhat dramatic use of cosmetics, with dark eyeliner and lipstick and sometimes a preference for enhancing any sort of pallor one may have

- Hair an unnatural shade of black, white, pre-Raphaelite red, or a color not found in the "natural" range of hair colors

- Skulls, bats, spider webs, gargoyles, and coffins appearing as a recurring motif in clothing, jewelry, home decor items, or just about anything, really

- Absinthe, because of its associations with artistic inspiration and decadence

- An interest in all or many things morbid and darkly fantastic

- An overwhelming fondness for all things relating to Halloween, perhaps including a firm belief that Jack-o'-lanterns are a perfectly valid decoration year-round

- A fondness for reading, especially works concerned with vampires, witches, monsters, folklore, the occult, or just the horror genre overall

- Striped stockings and tights

- Top hats and long black veils

  Black trench coats, opera coats, and velvet cloaks

- Music in a minor key, music that conjures strong emotions, and music that evokes longing and loss

- Ghost stories and haunted houses

- The films of Tim Burton

- Poetry of a gloomy nature

- Stormy nights, flickering candles, and photos taken in graveyards

- Corsets, bustles, and cravats with darkly bejeweled stick-pins

- Lace gloves, velvet chokers, silver-headed walking sticks, and poison rings

- Dark velvet and torn black lace

- Old horror movies in flickering black and white.

Are all Goths interested in every last one of those things? Good heavens, no. But those are some of the recurring markers of a gothy mindset, signs that you may be more spookily inclined than you might have realized. The sharp-eyed among you will note that "feeling depressed," "cutting oneself," or "hurting others" are *nowhere* on that list. All of those phrases reflect common misconceptions about what Goths are like, and all of them are wrong. Goths, by their very nature, are more willing to acknowledge feelings of sadness than other people, but that doesn't mean that you have to be sad all the time or hurt yourself to be considered a Goth.

So what if you have suddenly realized that you have gothy tendencies? Does this mean you should rush out, buy an anthology of the works of Edgar Allan Poe and the collected episodes of *The Addams Family* and start amassing an all-black wardrobe? Wellllllllll, only if you really want to. If those are things that you wanted to do before reading this book, then by all means, go forth and do them. But don't feel that you have to. Having interests in common with a particular subculture doesn't mean that you have to declare yourself a part of it. There's no Secret Goth Cabal that monitors who purchases black eyeliner and vampire novels and sends them the secret membership application once they have accumulated enough Goth Points. Which leads us neatly to the very next section. . .

The difference between being a Goth, a NotAGoth, and not being a Goth yourself but being Goth-friendly

Wait, the difference between being a Goth and a NotAGoth? You may be wondering what on earth a NotAGoth is. You see, there are people who are extremely Goth, people who are perfect examples of spookiness or are legendary icons in our dark and gloomy subculture, who want nothing to do with the label of Goth. People who, if asked about it, will say they don't consider themselves Goths and don't want to be labeled as such. (Sometimes they will say this quite vehemently.) They are NotAGoths. However, NotAGoth is something of a long-standing inside joke in the Goth subculture. Time and time again it seems that the people who are very obviously Goth are the ones who proclaim they are Not Goth At All the loudest, which has led the rest of the Goth community to nod wisely and say, "Oh yes, that is the true and final stage of being a Goth. You become so Goth you are NotAGoth." Examples of this phenomenon include some of the top icons of the Gothic music genre, such as Siouxsie Sioux, Peter Murphy (of Bauhaus), Robert Smith (of The Cure), and Andrew Eldritch (of The Sisters of Mercy). (If you haven't heard of those bands but are interested in the Goth subculture, do yourself a favor and give them a listen.) Andrew Eldritch rather infamously booted a supporting act off of a tour because he felt they were "too Goth."

So what should you do when presented with these NotAGoth types? Should you argue with them, point out all the ways in which they are extremely *gawthick*? No. Just smile, nod, and let them be. In some cases, people proclaim they are not part of something because they feel they've moved beyond such labels. Maybe they once were Goth, and maybe they still have interests that would define them as part of the subculture, but they don't feel that those interests are the most prominent parts of who they are now. (This is sometimes also known as the "Oh yes, I used to be a Goth, but I've moved beyond it" argument and is frequently spouted by people who, for whatever reason, have bought into the notion that Goth is a phase, something to grow out of. There will be more on that notion later.)

Some NotAGoths don't feel they are Goths, no matter what anyone else thinks. In their minds, they may have a lot in common with Goths, but not enough to earn that label for themselves. The Lady of the Manners's dear husband is one of these sorts of creatures; he says that even though he has a dark and acerbic sense of humor, and even though he prefers a wardrobe of somber shades, and even though his artwork tends to feature monstrous creatures, he is not a *big enough* fan of the music, of vampire novels, of fancy clothing to be called a Goth. No matter how much of a spooky and beribboned dark cupcake his wife is. To which, again, the Lady of the Manners just smiles and lets him be. If people don't want to consider themselves Goths, there's nothing wrong with that. If we want it to be okay to embrace the Goth label, we have to extend the same kindness to those who would reject it. Trying to categorize other people is a harmless diversion that almost everyone indulges in; just make sure you treat others with the same courtesy and respect you want them to grant to you.

So what if you don't consider yourself a Goth and other people haven't tried to call you a Goth, but you do share some interests and seem to have a fair number of friends who are Goths? Why yes, you would be considered Goth-friendly, and oh goodness, does the Goth community need more people who *are* Goth-friendly. In the very best cases, people who are Goth-friendly are the ones who look "completely normal," whatever that really means, but will speak up in defense when other, more closed-minded people make disparaging comments about one of the spooky and black-clad. Someone who will gently try to point out that no, Goths aren't a danger to themselves or others, and they aren't all depressed or creepy. People who, if pressed, will talk about the interests they share with those weird Goth types. Does this mean that Goth-friendly equals being some sort of activist for the equal treatment for the spooky and black-clad? No. (Though the Lady of the Manners isn't going to stop you if you do want to take that up as a cause.) What it means is that the Goth-friendly are people who treat Goths just as they treat everyone else. (Yes, the Lady of the Manners does come back to that core point rather a lot. But it is a good point!)

Some people who consider themselves to be Goth-friendly are that way because they used to be more active in the Goth world but for whatever reason, they've drifted away from the subculture. They still like certain aspects of it, and a Bauhaus or Dead Can Dance reunion tour will almost certainly drag them out of wherever they've been hiding, but the Goth subculture isn't as big a part of their lives as it might have been at one point. For them, the time they spent closely identifying with Goth really was a phase. A phase they think of with affection, but nevertheless consider a phase. But just because they've moved on doesn't mean they think disdainfully of those who still identify with that world of gloom and black velvet. After all, they probably still have a lot of friends who self-identify as Goth. Sure, there will probably be some good-natured teasing back and forth between the Goths and the lapsed Goths, but hopefully it's based on the mutual understanding of each other's quirks and interests.

Something that Goths with non-Goth friends absolutely must keep in mind is that they should not try to "convert" them. Oh yes, the Lady of the Manners understands all too well the urge to do a complete makeover on a "normal on the outside" friend, to treat him as your very own dress-up doll, take him out, and flaunt your handiwork. But if your friend says he'd rather not be your before-and-after project, respect that. Friendship isn't about setting out to change a person into someone completely different just because you want him to be a better match or an accessory for you. Yes, over time your friend will possibly come to share more interests with you (if sometimes in a tangential way), but that works both ways. Your friends' interests will also rub off on you, giving all of you even more things to stay up all night talking about. Choosing your friends solely based on how Goth you think they are (or how much time they spend playing the same video games as you, how big a sports fan, how attractive they are, and so on) is more than a touch shallow. Friends should make you laugh, make you think, and bring new ideas and experiences to your life, not be some sort of collection of clones of you. If that's what you want, it would probably be easier to just stay home and talk to your mirror. The Lady of the Manners thinks that would get rather boring very quickly, but if that's what you really want, she's not going to stop you. Shake her head rather sadly, yes, but stop you, no.

The age gap (also known as, "Am I too old for this?")

Remember a few pages ago when the Lady of the Manners mentioned how Goth is frequently viewed as a teenage phase? As if Goth were something that only interested young'ns flailing and searching around for who they are and what it all means? That an interest in all things dark and macabre, that refusing to act as if the world is at all times a happy and shiny place, are childish passions only to be indulged for a short time until one "grows up" and takes one's place in a gray and dreary world devoid of magic, dark sparkle, and whimsy?

To say that the Lady of the Manners disagrees with that line of thinking is putting things very mildly. Oh, the Lady of the

Manners does understand where the idea comes from—make no mistake about that. The people who are frequently *most* visible in their dark plumage and finery tend to be those who don't have to worry about making a "good impression" on a potential employer. Adults, who *should* know better, often still fear that they must hide who they truly are and blend in with the other denizens of the everyday world to make a living. And those of us who make no attempt to blend in are frequently assumed to be younger than we are. A few years ago, a new-ish coworker of the Lady of the Manners struck up a conversation with her about her appearance. Eyeing her black-frilled skirts, black velvet jacket, stripy tights, and top hat, the coworker asked, "So is this a Goth thing?" When the Lady of the Manners cheerfully acknowledged this, the coworker went on to say, "Oh, well you're probably too young to know about this, but Goth actually got started back in the '80s, when I was a teen . . ."

At this point, the Lady of the Manners gently interrupted him and asked how old he thought she was. The nice coworker had assumed that the Lady of the Manners was a good decade younger than she really was. While the Lady of the Manners takes no small amount of glee in the fact that slathering on sunblock and avoiding daylight whenever possible does help preserve a youthful appearance, the truth of the matter is that her coworker had fallen into the trap of assuming that no one over the age of twenty-five could possibly be a Goth.

So why do people think there's a "use-by" date on being a Goth? Perhaps because people think Goths are either moody teenagers in black or mid-twenties clubgoers in glossy vinyl outfits, and that being a Goth is something you grow out of, not into. Which, if you stop to think about it, is preposterous.

There are those who didn't come to the Goth subculture in

their teenage years, people who have slowly developed a fondness for the dark, gloomy beauty and whimsy that the world has to offer, who, possibly, weren't aware that there was a whole subculture and philosophy they could call home. Because of the stereotypical view that Goth is only for those in their teens and early twenties, these people worry that they shouldn't explore this world of dark enchantments, that at most they can dabble in it every year at Halloween or when the fashion industry decrees that inky-hued velvet and black nail polish are in style for a season. The Lady of the Manners feels particularly wistful about these adults who think they can't express themselves the way they want to, and encourages them to consider Goth something more than a mere costume they can put on once a year. However, the Lady of the Manners will admit there are some pitfalls awaiting "old" people exploring the Goth subculture for the first time, things they should be wary of if they don't want to look like they're trying too hard.

Warning the First: Age-appropriate looks, please. Don't draw *all* over your face with eyeliner, and don't feel you must wear head-to-toe "I am the Queen of the Night" spooky vampire clothes* that

would make you into a walking billboard for certain mall stores or that look like they originally came from a plastic-bagged costume kit. Being a Goth of a certain age means that you probably know the difference between what is an appropriate outfit for a night club and what is an appropriate outfit for work.

Warning the Second: Just because you've decided you're a Goth does not mean you must act depressed, languid, or mysterious all the time. This is a mindset that, er, younger Goths fall prey to sometimes; being older should mean you're a bit wiser about this sort of thing. Goth is a subculture and (for some) a way of life, not an emotional template.

Warning the Third: Do some research. A certain amount of "I wear black because it mirrors my tormented soul!" and "The world is a bleak place! I have written a poem about it/these song lyrics express my deep emotions!" posturing and drama is to be expected from younglings and teens who are floundering about trying to determine who they are. But as an adult taking part in the Goth subculture, you should be a bit more aware of what has drawn you to it. Is it an interest in the occult? In Gothic and Romantic literature? A fondness for dark-colored and antique clothing? If you are able to articulate why you have decided

*Unless, of course, you've been dressing that way for years and years anyway and it's become a personal trademark of yours. The Lady of the Manners's daily wardrobe includes petticoats and a top hat, so she's not going to tell you that you can't wear such things. Just make sure you're wearing the outfit, as opposed to it wearing you.

to explore this dark side, even if just to yourself, you won't feel quite as taken aback when someone your own age blurts out, "Oh, I had a Goth phase too. I grew out of it . . ."

Warning the Fourth: Do not become a Goth just to meet sexy death chicks and brooding boys. Don't take this as an affront, but the Lady of the Manners has seen far too many people (of all age groups, to be fair) decide they want to be Goth so they can meet attractive people dressed in black. If this is your whole reason for joining the Goth subculture, perhaps you should rethink things. Also, while there is absolutely nothing wrong with dating someone younger than you, particularly if all of your romances are with people much younger than you, be prepared for gossip and possibly unkind comments.

The joy of growing older is that one becomes more comfortable with oneself, which means not needing to prove how Goth you are by how many Goth stereotypes you live up to. There's nothing wrong with not wearing all black 24/7, or deciding that getting enough sleep so you can go to work the next morning is more important than staying out all night at the club; it doesn't make you less of a Goth, it makes you your own person.

With age comes wisdom; that's the theory, anyway. With age also comes the probability that a person will be more settled in life and able to devote more time, energy, and money to hobbies. While the general public associates Goth with depressed teenagers, many Goths are in their late twenties to thirties or even (gasp) older and have decent enough jobs that they sometimes have the spare funds to splurge on really extravagant Goth toys or clothes. Also, ElderGoths are generally smart enough to realize that appearing on sensationalist TV shows will not do them (or the subculture) any favors. They (hopefully) know the difference between something cool and something that is strictly a marketing gimmick aimed at weird people in black. But the best part of being older and being a Goth? Well-meaning people eventually stop telling you that "it's a phase" you'll "grow out of."

Do you have to be spooky every day?

On the list of strange assumptions that people have about Goths, there is the belief that Goths are spooky creatures of darkness all the time. That we sleep in coffins, that we don't do anything unless there is a gothy aspect to it, and that we always, *always* wear black and a face full of makeup. The Lady of the Manners is sure the Goths reading this have encountered people who make this assumption: coworkers or classmates who express astonishment if you wear something other than inky hues. "Wow, you're not wearing all black!" they'll exclaim, as if you hadn't picked out your own clothes. Many of the Lady of the Manners's friends are fond of replying to such comments, in their best startled tone, "I'm not?! Dammit, this was a black shirt when I left the house!" or some other slightly sarcastic response that should cause the commenter to realize the observation was perhaps just a smidge on the obvious side. While it may come as a surprise to some readers, the Lady of the Manners supports gently sarcastic responses to clueless and obvious statements made by non-Goths. The Lady of the Manners doesn't want you to call people idiots, but there's nothing wrong with carefully pointing out that perhaps someone's brain wasn't entirely engaged when she opened her mouth. However, after you point out (in a mildly sarcastic manner) that the comment was kind of silly, you might hear, "But I thought Goths wore black all the time?" Be willing to explain that this isn't actually a requirement, and that the Secret Goth Cabal won't banish you for wearing other colors. (There isn't really a Secret Goth Cabal. You knew that, yes? But it's a long-standing joke, along with Goth Points and getting your Goth card stamped each time you do something particularly gothy. Take, as an example, one of the Lady of the Manners's recent quiet nights at home. She sat around with black hair dye on her head, reading a vampire novel and listening to The Sisters of Mercy. This earned her many, many nonexistent Goth Points.)

The Lady of the Manners isn't really sure why people expect Goths to be very Goth all the time. After all, no one expects sports fans to be all about the sport of their choice for every minute of their lives, do they? People aren't surprised when knitting enthusiasts wear something other than hand-knitted creations. But something about the idea that Goths don't spend all their free time writing morose poetry and lurking about in cemeteries seems to escape a lot of people.

Of course, it doesn't help matters that there are those in our spooky little subculture who . . . how can the Lady of the Manners phrase this? Who believe the hype, who believe that you must be hard-core ooky-spooky Goth all the time. There is a difference between someone who believes that every day is Halloween and someone who thinks that washing off the eyeliner and watching cartoons while wearing pj's means you're not a Real Goth. This latter type of person tends to pick hobbies and interests based on whether they increase the darkling-creature-of-the-night persona, as opposed to whether the hobbies are interesting. These same sorts are usually the ones making lofty pronouncements to their friends, like, "You can't be a Real Goth if you like that." (And yes, you can hear the capital letters in Real Goth very well when this sort of person says it.)

"You can't be a Real Goth if . . ." Oh, please—what rubbish. There is no activity, interest, or item of clothing that will get one summarily thrown out of the world of Goth. Really. No, not even liking country music. Because, please, if Johnny Cash wasn't a forefather of Goth, then no one was, and we should all just give up any notion of this subculture right now. The Lady of the Manners knows of DJs at Goth clubs who delight in playing non-Goth music in the middle of their sets and watching the dance floor fill up. (Those same DJs will cackle delightedly at the Gother-than-thou types who promptly throw temper tantrums when non-Goth music starts blaring out, because it seems to be a law of nature that the person thrown into a tizzy by hearing "SexyBack" is likeliest to request a song by a band the DJ played not fifteen minutes before.)

"You can't be a Real Goth if . . ." what? If you spend your week-ends hiking and camping? If you are a devout (and obviously open-minded) Christian? If you're in the military? If you don't spend every waking moment in velvet and frills? If you love going to Disneyland? If you don't like the movies of Tim Burton, if horror novels scare you, if you don't feel the need to paint your bedroom black or blood red? You see, there is no way to complete the "You can't be a Real Goth if . . ." statement without it sounding ridiculous. Yes, for many people Goth is a core part of who they are, but it isn't the *only* thing they are. While their dark and spooky mindset and tastes probably add a shadowy tinge to just about everything they do, they don't only do things that are on some sort of pre-approved Goth activity list. (Another thing that doesn't really exist, much like the Secret Goth Cabal.)

The people who tend to spout off the Real Goth nonsense, or who believe you must be spooktacular all the time, are gener-ally very insecure. They're worried that someone, somewhere, is judging them, finding them lacking, and that it's only a matter of time before a member of the nonexistent Secret Goth Cabal swoops down and exposes them for the gothy fraud they are. It seems that the only way these sorts of people can make themselves feel better is to pose as all-knowing members of that nonexistent Secret Goth Cabal and pass disapproving judgment on others.

Why you shouldn't believe everything you read on the Internet, including those silly quizzes

Speaking of passing disapproving judgment on others, it's time to talk about the Internet! Oh, all right, the Internet isn't entirely about passing disapproving judgment on others; sometimes it's about trying to make yourself seem cooler than you really are.

Wait, wait, come back here. The Lady of the Manners is joking, of course. The Internet has been a huge boon to Goth culture, allowing people of a dark and eccentric nature to reach out across geographical boundaries and communicate with like-minded souls. So what if you're the only Goth in your small town, or if no one around you understands your interests? Thanks to the Internet, with its blogs, message boards, LiveJournal, MySpace, Facebook, and every other social networking site, isolated Goths can find others like themselves and have a sense of community and belonging. There are countless Goth-themed social groups online, with more springing up all the time. These forums and message boards can be centered on events, musicians, brands of makeup, TV shows, specific aspects of Gothdom—just about anything, really. Not only has the Internet made it easier for Goths around the world to truly become a global community, it has also helped the subculture grow as independent artists are able to reach a wider audience, isolated Goths are able to find clothing and merchandise that appeals to their non-mainstream tastes, and people can plan and organize large events to bring members of the black-clad tribe together for an always all-too-short time of socializing and fun.

But (and you knew there was a cautionary "but" coming because you're very clever) there is a dark and not-good side of the Internet Goth community (as opposed to the dark and good side, because that *is* what Goth is all about). People seem to forget that there is no elite board of fact-checkers that oversees the Internet and that just because something is posted online doesn't make it true. People can go online, make up whatever outlandish story they want, and post it somewhere to be read. And you can guarantee that there will be someone, somewhere, who will believe that outlandish story and repeat it to others. Of course, the same thing has been going on for ages and ages, long before the Internet existed. But the Internet sped things up, so to speak. Now, instead of "I heard this from my cousin's best friend's ex-boyfriend, who heard it from one of his bandmate's girlfriends," stories that should probably be greeted with a skeptically raised eyebrow are introduced with, "I read this online . . ." (That sentence frequently ends, the Lady of the Manners adds wryly, with the words "on MySpace.")

Yes, as the old saying goes, on the Internet, no one knows you're a dog. You can be anyone and say anything on the Internet. The Lady of the Manners has read journals and forum posts from people's pets and imaginary friends. Why, even the Lady of the Manners's very own beloved fanged toy bunny has a blog (that the Lady of the Manners's parents apparently read faithfully). What the Lady of the Manners is trying to get across here is that just because an online post makes someone come across as the gothiest thing since the creation of black velvet, that doesn't make it true. There are role-playing forums and message boards, and even huge games such as *World of Warcraft*, *City of Heroes*, or *Second Life*, where the whole point is that everyone posts in character. These online environments are based on the idea that people like to be someone or something they're not in everyday life, which is fantastic. But there are people who don't want to limit their pretending to venues where everyone is in on the fantasy. Instead, those people create whole selves, entire separate personas complete with pictures (found and "borrowed" from all over), and claim these identities are real. It isn't difficult at all to create an idealized version of who you want to be and live a fictional life on the Internet. No, what seems to be the hard part is seamlessly maintaining that fictional life and not being found out. From what the Lady of the Manners has seen, people who claim to be someone other than who they are always eventually lose the thread; they have to juggle too many different stories and eventually get tangled up in their own make-believe life. The Lady of the Manners isn't sure why those sorts of people feel the need to represent themselves as someone entirely different. Is it because they feel no one would be interested in who they really are? Is it because they feel their own lives aren't exciting or dramatic enough, and want to make things more interesting? Who knows? But ultimately, the Lady of the Manners has never seen that sort of thing end well. People pretending to be something other than who and what they are risk betraying the people who believed in them when the truth comes out. Perhaps this is not a huge and life-shattering level of betrayal, and the people with the fictional life will frequently try to defend their actions with claims of "It wasn't hurting anyone!" but no one likes being lied to, even in minor ways.

Does the Lady of the Manners mean you should constantly be suspicious of everyone you meet and everything you read online?

No, of course not. But a healthy dose of skepticism is probably a good idea. Don't take everything at face value. Ask questions, and try to trace stories or comments back to their sources. But! Even if someone's life seems to be preposterous or outlandish, remember there is a chance that you are reading the unvarnished, unadulterated truth. There are people who have had improbable things happen to them; of course, those people are usually well aware that not everyone will believe them. Sometimes they themselves have problems believing the things that have happened to them. The Lady of the Manners has seen her fair share of unbelieving e-mails insinuating that she isn't real or is a forty-something man dwelling in his parents' basement. (For the record, the Lady of the Manners is quite real and is an eccentric lady in her early forties living in her very own house with her husband and cats. Whether you believe her is entirely up to you.)

There is a very fuzzy line between giving people the benefit of the doubt and thinking the best of them, and not trusting anything you read online ever again. The best advice the Lady of the Manners can give about the whole thing is to double and triple-check anything having to do with money, and to try and keep a sense of humor about it all.

Oh, and about a sense of humor . . . you don't really think that any quiz or survey found online has any bearing on how Goth you are, do you? Or any bearing on anything but how much amusement someone found in creating a multiple-choice test and putting it up somewhere? Quizzes and surveys and memes (or at least, what an awful lot of people call memes, because that term is shockingly misused) should be treated as nothing more than light entertainment, not as pronouncements graven in stone about what sort of person you are. Do not work yourself into a tizzy if some online quiz doesn't validate your gothness or doesn't give you the answer or picture you want to associate with yourself. And for heaven's sake, do not start worrying about whether you're a Real Goth because of an online quiz. For that matter, try to banish the phrase "Real Goth" from your mind and instead concentrate on being your own person. If being your own person happens to involve wearing black-hued finery and wishing you were a member of the Addams Family or other things that make you want to claim the label of Goth, then so be it.

TWO

I'm Not a Goth, But I Have Some Questions About Them...

Common misconceptions about Goths

You've seen them, those rather pale people wearing flamboyant, exotic black clothing. Perhaps you've noticed that your child prefers a more . . . monochromatic wardrobe than you expected or is starting to show a marked fondness for black eyeliner and dark lipstick. Or maybe a coworker apparently owns nothing but somber velvet and jewel tones, accessories with an equally dark sense of humor, and decorates his workspace with toy bats and coffins.

Because you're clever, it dawns on you that those people just might be Goths. But you're not quite sure what that means; don't those sorts all think they're vampires? Or feel depressed and contemplate suicide all the time? Or maybe they're in a cult?

No.

Goths don't all think they're vampires (although vampires are a key fashion influence); they're not all depressed and suicidal (but a lot of art from the various Gothic movements involves strong emotions of all types); and if Goths are in a cult, then so is every single fan of an organized sport, knitting, or Oprah Winfrey.

Goth is not a cult but a movement and a subculture that has been around in one form or another for centuries. So don't automatically assume that, just because someone is wearing black clothes, she's some sort of cultist. She almost certainly isn't, and if she is, the Lady of the Manners is willing to bet her collection of parasols that her being in a cult has nothing to do with being a Goth. The Goth subculture is just that, a subculture, with no reli-

gious requirements. Sure, some aspects of the Goth subculture are laden with occult trappings (candles, incense, strange images, odd and old books, ghost stories, tarot cards), but that doesn't mean that to be a Real Goth, one must check the "Other" box for religion and list "Spoooooooky."

As a matter of fact, one's choice of religious belief does not automatically make one Goth. The Lady of the Manners personally knows Goths who are Jewish, Christian, Protestant, Catholic, Wiccan, Mormon, Buddhist, and yes indeed, even one or two Satanists. The Lady of the Manners also knows many, many Goths who are agnostics or atheists, or who are just keeping an open mind about the whole topic of religion but still willing to enter into spirited (no pun intended) discussions of belief, faith, and religion. Of course, "spirited" should not mean belligerent or antagonistic, but the Lady of the Manners is all too aware that discussions about religion can turn heated even when there aren't strange black-clad people involved.

So where does this strange assumption that Goth equals Satanist come from? Well, the Satanists the Lady of the Manners knows tend to dress in black and be very decadent and a little extreme in personality. Just like most Goths. The Lady of the Manners doesn't have to explain to all of you that real, honest-to-darkness Church of Satan Satanism is in no way involved with raising demons, sacrificing humans or animals, and is nothing at all like TV and movies would have you think, does she? No, she thought not. "Satanist," much like "Goth," is frequently used by the media as shorthand for "creepy," "freaky," or someone who is "just not right." The only problem is that this shorthand isn't really accurate and just adds fuel to the unnecessary and unwarranted paranoia about both Satanists and Goths. While the Lady of the Manners knows that the complete strangers who walk up to her and offer to pray for (or with) her mean well, it's still a little disconcerting that some people believe they can discern a person's spiritual preferences with a mere glance. Just because someone is wearing extravagant black clothing or items with skulls, bats, or coffins on them doesn't mean she's in need of spiritual guidance.

You may be thinking, "But what about the vampire thing?" Yes, the Lady of the Manners can tell that was on your mind, so don't try to deny it. You're right, many people in the Goth subculture look like they've stepped off the set of a vampire movie. (Either one of the modern, action-adventure ones filled with aggressive music and fight scenes or one of the type that strives for an air of antique menace.) And yes, the subculture sprang up in the wake of Bauhaus's song "Bela Lugosi's Dead." But do Goths really believe they're vampires? Gracious, no. Many Goths like enjoying or dressing like characters from vampire books, movies, and games, and some even like Count Chocula breakfast cereal, but they don't really think that they're undead creatures of the night. In fact, if confronted with a person who claims to be a vampire, most Goths would suggest that this person needs to get out more, look for a way to flee the conversation, or just start snickering. In fact, the Lady of the Manners has been asked for advice on how to deal with people who really do think they are undead creatures of the night. The Lady of the Manners suggested that the best way to deal with those people is to play along with the whole idea in the most exaggerated manner possible. Constantly ask them about what life as a vampire is like; ask when and how they became a vampire. Ask them for help with history homework, and if they reply that they haven't been around that long, ask if they know another vampire who has been.

Of course, there *is* a flourishing vampire (or vampyre—pick your spelling) subculture, and at first glance, it's difficult to tell the Goths apart from the vampires. (From what the Lady of the Manners understands, while the vampires are interested in and strongly identify with the blood-sucking creatures of legend, they don't actually believe that they are immortal undead creatures of the night.) There is some crossover between the Goth and vampire worlds, but members of both communities become very cross if they are stamped with the wrong subcultural label. Most Goths think the vampire types need to get a life and stop playing pretend, while the vampire types tend to think that the Goths need to get over themselves.

However, with that said, walking up to a black-clad, pale, and interesting creature and asking him if he's a vampire is . . . not as funny as you might think. Even if he was a vampire, why in Dracula's name would he tell you?

Another cliché attributed to Goths is that they're all depressed and/or suicidal, which is absolutely silly; Goths are no more depressed and/or suicidal than anyone else. Wearing a lot of black and searching for beauty in dark or unexpected places doesn't make one depressed; it makes one, in the words of Lydia from the movie *Beetlejuice*, "strange and unusual." The world isn't always a happy, shiny place, and Goths not only acknowledge that fact but also embrace it in order to defuse it. Over-dramatizing things that worry or frighten you is a way to lampoon them; death happens to everyone (even those who think they're vampires), so why not explore the historical and societal trappings of it by dressing like you've just come from a Victorian séance and are now on your way to a funeral? Goth is sometimes a way for people to say, "No, things aren't okay. But don't feel like you have to pretend they are; you're not alone." And while the stereotype of locking oneself in one's room to write tortured poetry about one's broken heart will always have a special place in the collective consciousness of Goths everywhere, very few of them actually adhere to that particular stereotype. (And even if they do, they probably don't show the poetry to anyone, anyway.)

The Lady of the Manners has always been bemused by the seemingly contradictory beliefs that Goths are full of woe and de-

---

A brief tangent: emo, much like Goth, is frequently used as a derisive label to indicate that someone is overwhelmingly depressed over nothing, is prone to self-harm as a form of expression, and "looks funny." The Lady of the Manners will admit that she frequently cannot tell which sullen-looking teens wearing black clothing, a lot of eye makeup, and elaborately styled asymmetrical hair are babygoths and which are emo kids. No, looking for bat or skull jewelry doesn't seem to help because some of the emo kids adorn themselves with that iconography too.

Just as the stereotypes and assumptions about Goth are wrong, so are the ones about the emo kids. No, they don't advocate hurting yourself. No, emo isn't a teen suicide cult. Emo, like Goth, is a subculture that sprung up around a particular subgenre of music. (Though the Lady of the Manners has heard stories that the whole emo label really started as an inside joke.) Just because someone decides to wear tight black jeans, have a hairstyle that involves hair dye and a lot of styling product, and listen to music that features (primarily) male vocalists shouting in a musical fashion over loud guitars does not mean that this person is never, ever happy. Perhaps more prone to wallowing in emotions of woe and anger than other people, but for cathartic reasons, not because this person won't or can't feel anything else.

There are many, many differences between Goth and emo, even if the casual observer can't spot them right away. But the core difference is that Goths are spooky, with an interest in a darker, more shadowy beauty, whereas emo kids are not as interested in such things and are perhaps more interested in writing long blog posts about what's cur-

spair and while away the hours by indulging in illicit pharmacology and degenerate acts. You don't really think that all Goths are drug fiends, do you? That if someone wears a lot of black and has a preference for eyeliner, she must be filling her every waking hour with unspeakable depravity? The Lady of the Manners hates to shatter your illusions, but that's not really how it is. Goths are no more prone to those sorts of behaviors than anyone else. After all, doesn't every after-school special feature some "normal"-looking blonde suburban teen getting mixed up with drugs? Goths do tend to be a bit

rently upsetting them. Not to mention the Lady of the Manners isn't entirely certain that anyone still embraces the emo label once the overwhelmingly emotional teen years are over. She could be wrong, but while Goth is very much a subculture for the generations, there is a reason the label of emo is usually followed by the word "kid." But, as the Lady of the Manners said, she could be wrong, and the current version of the emo subculture may grow into a cross-generational lifestyle, just like the Goth subculture has.

more open-minded and accepting about a lot of things, but there's no secret "You're not a Real Goth until you've performed these horrible and unnatural acts" checklist automatically mailed out by a Goth Cabal once someone purchases hair dye, black eyeliner, and some velvet clothing.

It is true that one of the core philosophies of the Goth subculture is decadence, but decadence does not automatically equal drug-filled orgies. No, Gothic decadence can, and usually does, mean candlelight, sumptuous food, luxurious fabrics, a spirited discussion of books, music, movies, and making mildly snippy comments about other members of the local Goth community who aren't present at that particular decadent event.

Can I comment on their clothing or makeup and ask if they make their own clothes?

They look so different! Of course you want to ask them about their elaborate makeup, their wildly colored hair, their hats, their very fancy funereal attire. And so you should! But walking up to someone and asking, "So what's with the outfit?" is a tad abrupt, and you don't want to be a pest or annoy the black-clad person who is (presumably) a creature of the night. So what should you keep in mind before you start asking questions?

If you go up to a gothy-type person and compliment him on his lovely costume, you might notice a faint flash of something close to irritation cross his face. It's not that he doesn't appreciate your compliment, it's that "costume" is a loaded word to those of the Goth persuasion. Costume subtly implies that we're pretending to be something we aren't, that our carefully chosen apparel is part of a facade we're hiding behind, and that we're dressed like that to get attention. For the majority of the spooky and shadow-clad, that's simply not true. We're not dressing up as someone or something different; we're expressing our interests and dressing in the way that we prefer. Would you go up to someone wearing a uniform jersey for a sports team and compliment her on her costume? Probably not; you'd just assume she was a sports fan. The same thing holds true for people dressed in elaborate and funereal clothing: they're not in costume and they're not seeking attention. They just have a different sense of aesthetics than you do.

Costume is also problematic because Goths can be very touchy about the ever-proliferating selection of "Goth" costumes that pop up every October. Those Halloween costumes err on the wrong side of cheesy (as just about any pre-packaged Halloween costume does), and the majority of them fall into the "Hi, I'm the Queen of the Bloodsucking Bimbos!" trap. Does this mean you shouldn't dress up in gothy finery on Halloween for fear of offending or upsetting any Goths you know? Oh, don't be silly. The Lady of the Manners has not only helped assorted coworkers dress up in a manner strikingly similar to her everyday wear, but she is gleeful (and a bit touched) that her own mom borrows from the Lady of the Manners's closets every October 31. The main objection most Goths have to "Goth costumes" is that they are very obviously *costumes*: shoddily made, less-than-ideal fabrics, and almost entirely lacking in the elegant whimsy department. While Goth has firm roots in the swampy territories of kitsch and B movie horror, that doesn't mean the sight of someone in badly applied "spooooooky" makeup, ill-fitting panne velvet, and a polyester vampire cloak doesn't make Goths everywhere cringe. We Goths cringe because, at the core of it, we still faintly worry that people are going to look at those dressed in chain-store Halloween costumes and assume they're the real thing and represent the sum total of the Goth sub-culture, and we're all going to be dismissed as crazy people who need to go outside and get a life. Which is far from the truth, as you know, since you've read this far.

There's one final catch to the idea of "costume," and it's one that seems to occur to everyone who knows a Goth. At some point, when the calendar draws close to Halloween, the suggestion, "Oh, you should dress up like a normal person for Halloween! Wear jeans and a T-shirt and no makeup! That would be really funny!" is made.

(The Lady of the Manners needs to pause, press a limp hand to her brow, and sigh forlornly. Just give her a minute.)

Look, the Lady of the Manners knows that every person who has ever made this suggestion to her has meant well and genuinely thought it was a novel idea. The key phrase in that sentence was "every person," by the way. Yes, the "dress up like a normal person!" suggestion is one that the Lady of the Manners and every other Goth has heard over and over and over. You know what? Some Goths have even followed through on that suggestion, and that's great. The Lady of the Manners has not and probably won't ever. Because for her and countless other Goths, Halloween is a special day to dress even more elaborately, a chance to dress the way we long to in our black velvet hearts. Or it's a chance to take those spooky clichés and, on a scale of one to ten, ramp them up to thirteen, to revel in imagery of glamorous vampires and witches, and to poke gentle fun at ourselves. (Of course, we run the risk of people not quite getting the joke; one Halloween, the Lady of the Manners wore elaborate black and white Victorian-tinged finery to work. One of her coworkers, walking up to her from behind, said, "Jillian, it doesn't count as a costume if you wear your regular clothes." Then, the Lady of the Manners turned around and her coworker was treated to a full view of the stage-blood-drenched front of the white blouse and fangs. The coworker took a step back and said, "Oh.")

When you do ask a Goth about her clothing and she replies with something like, "I look like this all the time," for heaven's sake, do not reply, "No, really?" or otherwise suggest disbelief. This happens to the Lady of the Manners all the time, and it's quite aggravating. The Lady of the Manners understands that to non-Goths, items such as stripy tights, petticoats, or top hats are not everyday wear. But for some of us, they are. When you respond with, "No, really?" or other doubting comments, you are essentially accusing us of lying to you. Oh, the Lady of the Manners is sure that's not how you mean it, but how else are we to interpret that sort of comment? Certainly there are those in every subculture or community who find amusement in making up fibs and stories in response to well-intentioned questions from complete strangers, but the majority of Goths (and other people) answer such questions in a truthful manner. So when a questioner responds to our answer with a doubting comment, we (quite naturally) feel a little resentful. If you have already made up your mind as to why we look the way we do, why on earth are you bothering to ask us about it?

Another touchy topic related to asking Goths about their clothing is, well, the people who feel compelled to reach out and touch or pet the gothy finery without asking permission. You would be surprised how often this happens, and the Lady of the Manners is somewhat bewildered as to why. One theory is that the more elaborate and fancy our outfits, the more we Goths look like interesting dolls; it seems many people's instinctive reaction to interesting dolls is an impulse to examine the clothing. Another theory is that Goth clothing is usually made from interestingly textured fabrics. Velvets, silks, lace, PVC—all materials that make people want to reach out and touch them. Velvet jackets, petticoat-fluffed skirts, and feather-adorned hats all seem to have a magnetic draw for people who don't encounter such finery on a daily basis. (The Lady of the Manners has discovered that ladies of a certain age—oh fine, little old ladies—are the sort of people who have no qualms whatsoever about patting or fluffing full skirts worn by someone else. This well-meaning invasion of privacy can probably be explained by the fact that the little old ladies are so delighted to see someone wearing petticoats that they just have to gently rustle the tulle and chiffon, but it's still a little unnerving and rude.)

The Lady of the Manners would like to think that this is an obvious bit of advice but still feels compelled to state it very clearly: always ask permission before touching someone you don't know! Just because someone looks different or exotic (or pregnant—how often have you heard a pregnant lady complain about random people touching her belly?) does not mean he or she has escaped from a petting zoo. If you are talking to a person who makes it clear he does not want to have his clothing or hair touched, please honor his wishes. Do not argue with him (no matter how good-naturedly you try to present your reasons for wanting to touch him), and do not completely ignore his wishes and start grabbing at him anyway. Just because someone has pink hair or is wearing fluffy skirts or has interesting tattoos does not mean that she does not need personal space or privacy.

Just as it is important to ask permission before you touch someone, it is also important to ask first before taking someone's photo. The Lady of the Manners realizes that in this modern age of camera phones, asking a stranger's permission before imitating the paparazzi probably seems a trifle quaint. But the Lady of the Manners is quite serious about it. Just because you have the ability to take a photo of someone doesn't mean they want you to. The Lady of the Manners has been unwittingly photographed by strangers while walking down the street (in various countries, no less), waiting in line at Disneyland, and out for a fancy dinner with her dear husband. In every one of those situations, if the person who desired a photo had just come up and asked first, the Lady of the Manners probably would have acquiesced. But there is something not only disconcerting, but annoying and slightly upsetting, about being distracted from what one thought was a private dinner by the sight of someone aiming a camera phone in one's direction and snapping away.

The Lady of the Manners can just hear you saying, "But what if they say no?" Well, then, they say no, and you will just have to live without a photo of that person. Mind you, most of the time, if you ask politely, you will indeed get your photo op. The Lady of the Manners is always amused by people who stop her and ask to take her photo; when she has asked the photo snappers why they want to take her photo, she has gotten responses as varied as, "Because my kid dresses kinda like you" to "Um, because you look, um, different?"

But even with those assorted pitfalls the Lady of the Manners has warned you about ("costume," "no, really," and touching or taking photos of people without permission), she absolutely wants to encourage you to ask questions of the gothy black-clad types you see around. Please! Feel free to ask them about their appearance! Feel free to ask them how they get their hair to look like that, or what brand of eyeliner they've so meticulously applied. Ask them about where they found such interesting clothing, or if they made it themselves; even ask them for advice or tips on sewing and DIY

> One autumn, after a week or two of what seemed like constant photo requests, the Lady of the Manners explained to the next eager photography student who approached her that while she'd be happy to let him take her photo, she suspected that his professor was going to see a number of photos of an eccentric Victorian Gothic lady, and perhaps he should find another random person on the street to photograph for his assignment.

fashion. (The Lady of the Manners has even been asked if she had any safety pins she could spare, as the questioner needed them to carry out some emergency clothing repairs.) Don't feel you should avoid speaking to any Goths you see, or that you can't ask them questions that you'd ask other people. They're not scary monsters or dangerous people. They merely look different from you.

Goths, while flamboyant, eccentric, strange, and unusual, are not that different from "regular people" when it comes to conversation. One obvious conversational difference is that many Goths will come across as shy or taciturn and perhaps not very interested in talking to you. It's because, on the whole, Goths are a bit . . . wary of entering into conversations with people they don't know very well. Not because they don't like other people, but because of a (hopefully unwarranted) worry that the strangers trying to strike up a conversation aren't actually interested in talking but, rather, are interested in amusing themselves by playing a brisk game of "taunt the weirdo." Or because (as many Goths have found) talking about their interests and lives outside of the work environment will garner them even more strange looks, or that they'll have to spend a very long time explaining why their interests and hobbies don't mean they're dangerous psychos. So don't be put off if the black-clad, pale, and interesting creature that you're trying to chat with doesn't respond to your conversational overtures with wild enthusiasm. Just keep your part of the conversation casual, friendly, and open.

Which means that walking up to that black-clad, pale, and interesting creature and commenting on her "costume," saying, "It isn't Halloween yet," or making comments about her casting a spell simply isn't really a fabulous way to break the ice. No matter how witty you think those comments are, chances are good that the poor Goths have heard it before. (Many, many times before. Probably as many times as a non-Goth has heard, "How about this weather?") If you're lucky, they'll take pity on you and either smile wanly or answer with, "Oh no, I dress this way all the time." If you're unlucky, they'll stare blankly at you, glare at you, or answer with a curt "no" and walk away. If you're very unlucky (or if the Goths haven't read any of the Lady of the Manners's words of advice), they may snarl insults at you or indulge in some outrageous behavior designed to scare you off. This doesn't mean you shouldn't ask them about their appearance; just don't feel you have to make a joke about it. There is nothing wrong with a direct, "That's a very interesting outfit/hair color/parasol/bag. Is it for a special occasion?"

Also, don't assume they're dressed like that because they want attention. Many Goths (the Lady of the Manners included) dress in an elaborate manner every day because that's what makes them happy. It's not a case of trying to elicit a reaction from strangers; it's a case of knowing who one is and being comfortable in one's skin. The Goths who express themselves through their wardrobe aren't doing it to draw attention to themselves; they're applying their preferred aesthetic and bringing the world around them closer to what they want it to be.

Finally, if you want to compliment the fabulously dressed creature you just saw, please do! If you particularly admire his hair, boots, lipstick, or anything about him, you shouldn't feel too shy to say so. Compliments are a lovely surprise, and the Lady of the Manners thinks the world would be a better place in general if people gave each other more sincere compliments, instead of shouting comments at each other and random strangers. (An aside: no, shouting "You're hot!" at someone is not actually a compliment. A general rule to follow is if you have to shout something at someone, it most likely will not be taken as a compliment but rather as harassment.)

A few words for the Goths reading this chapter

Look, you realize that most of the "norms" or "mundanes" who are going to approach you and ask about your "costume" or want to take your photo mean well, right? The majority of them aren't looking to harass you or cause a scene—they just want to know why you look different and "what's the deal?" with your appearance. Which means that you absolutely should not be snarly, snippy, or hostile with them for being brave enough to ask questions of a complete (and different-looking) stranger. (Oh, come on; you knew the Lady of the Manners was going to say that. Don't try to pretend you didn't.)

Mind you, this doesn't mean that you have to spend ages talking to them about Goth and what it is all about. A few quick words like, yes, your hair really is blue, or you're wearing a frock coat because you like it, are really all that you need to say. Also, if someone asks to touch your clothing or hair, you absolutely are not obligated to say yes. Don't recoil in horror or shriek; a calm "No,

> *Could we please try not to call non-Goths by terms like "norm" or "mundane" anymore? Yes, compared to the majority of our black-clad selves, the non-Goths appear pretty normal. But remember, not only does almost everyone certainly have hidden depths, but using those sorts of terms makes us no better than the people who call us "freaks." How can we hope to be treated politely if we don't do the same for them?*

I'd rather you didn't" is all you should need to say. (If the person doesn't pay attention to your polite refusal, move out of touching range and say, "No, please don't touch me." If the hint still doesn't register, repeat the "No, don't touch me" message in a much louder, sterner tone of voice. When all else fails, walk away, preferably to someplace well lit, with a lot of other people around.)

The Lady of the Manners realizes that her entire message to all of Gothdom can be distilled down to, "Look, just be polite, okay?" but feels that she must especially stress this with regard to non-Goths coming up and asking questions. Remember, most non-Goths are laboring under the misconception that Goths are at the very least depressed anti-social freaks and at the very worst blood-drinking, demon-worshipping deviants and fiends, neither of which is a particularly accurate stereotype. Being polite when someone asks a question about your appearance is, in many ways, the most shocking thing you could do. The questioner doesn't realize that you've probably been asked over and over if that's your real hair, why you are wearing a top hat, why you have all those tattoos and whatever do they mean? This is probably the first time the person asking has spoken to one of those vaguely spooky black-clad types. So try not to reinforce any of the negative stereotypes that may be rattling around in his or her head, no matter how many times you've been asked that sort of question.

Some of you may have come up with the oh-so-clever notion of treating those non-Goths the same way they're reacting to you. Pointing, exclaiming loudly at what they're wearing, taking photos of them, and other such shenanigans. The Lady of the Manners would like to take this opportunity to ever-so-gently point out that that sort of behavior is, well, dumb. Petty and pointless, really. The non-Goths you do that to probably aren't going to have a blinding realization like, "Wow, I bet it's just as annoying and exasperating when I act like this toward those weird people in the funny black clothes! I shall stop doing that immediately!" No, the non-Goths on whom you would inflict that sort of behavior would probably think, "Wow, those people in the funny black clothes are not only weird, but jackasses too! I guess all the bad things I've heard about them must be true!" Not to mention, why on earth would you want to waste your time harassing people and taking photos of them just because you may have been asked slightly foolish questions or had your photo taken? Don't you have better things to do with your time and energy? (Yes, you do, Snarklings. Don't even try to convince the Lady of the Manners that you don't. There are squillions of things that you could and should be doing instead of being an annoyance to others.)

A brief primer on how to behave and what to wear if you decide to explore the Goth scene with your spooky acquaintances

What if, after spending time talking to the Goths you know, you realize you'd like to socialize with them more often and want to ask to go to the local Goth club with them? To see them in their "natural habitat," as it were? There's nothing wrong with that; just understand that you will be a tourist in their world and need to be aware of some things.

Thing the First: Think long and hard about why you want to go to the local gothy nightspot. Is it to see friends of yours who are part of the scene? Is it because you're trying to decide if you want to become an active participant in the local Goth scene? Is it because you like the music? Great! All of those are good reasons, unlike, say, wanting to try to pick up one of those sexy death chicks or brooding boys because "everyone knows they're sluts." (Which is no more a truth in the Goth subculture than in the rest of the non-Goth population, by the way, just in case you were confused and believed such nonsense.) That is a bad reason. Be aware of the worlds of difference between good reasons and bad reasons.

Thing the Second: Try to dress to blend in. Black or dark clothing, if you please, and no sneakers, baseball caps, or bad attempts at extravagant eyeliner and black lipstick. A plain dress or a shirt and trousers in black or deep jewel tones are just fine. No, you won't be as elaborately dressed as many of the club attendees, but you're just visiting and trying not to stick out, so don't worry about it.

Thing the Third: Be very, very polite to the staff. Tip the bartenders. Do not ask the DJ if he has the latest Top 40 hit song. The staff will probably already be keeping a watchful eye on you, so do what you can to prove to them that their suspicions are unfounded.

Thing the Fourth: Don't be surprised if people stare or are obviously whispering about you, and don't get belligerent about it either. You are the odd one here, not the rest of the club patrons. Remember what the Lady of the Manners said about being polite to the staff? (Yes, you do; it was in the previous paragraph.) Well, you should also be very, very polite to the other people at the club, even if you think they're a bunch of freaks. After all, you decided to go to their club. Will you attract whispers and stares even if you pay attention to Thing the Second and dress to blend in? Maybe, maybe not. If you carry yourself in a manner that shows you're

comfortable with what you've decided to wear and with the surroundings, then probably not. But if you seem nervous, wary, or
disapproving, of course there will be odd glances cast your way.
People will wonder why you seem uneasy and may themselves be a
little wary about striking up a conversation with you.

But who knows? You may find that you enjoy going to the
dark and spooky places. You may even discover that the Goth
subculture feels like home to you and that you want to start exploring more of it. If you do (which the Lady of the Manners
approves of wholeheartedly, of course), don't feel that you have to
change your life overnight; also, don't try to turn yourself into an
exact replica of your Goth friends. While it has been said that
imitation is the sincerest form of flattery, using someone else as
a template for your new life isn't flattering—it's a bit creepy. But
do feel free to dabble in the darker aspects of life and fashion;
even if you decide it isn't for you, exploration of new things isn't
bad. Each and every person involved in the Goth scene had to
start somewhere, and some of those people were later bloomers (in a night-blooming garden, of course) than others. Besides,
popular culture and fashion borrow from the darker side of the
subcultural map all the time. Sometimes it leads people to discover a new interest in life, and sometimes it just means that

there's a wider selection of skull-festooned goodies for Goths to snap up at clearance sales.

Of course, even if you don't want to become one of these black-clad, pale, and interesting creatures, you still may be wondering if you should treat your gothy acquaintances carefully and make sure never to tease or poke fun at their spooky quirks. Of course not—don't be silly. Goths, by and large, have a pretty good sense of humor and are quite willing to turn it on themselves and their chosen subculture. The Lady of the Manners firmly believes that if you don't see the ridiculousness inherent in dressing like you've escaped from a Hammer horror movie or choosing accessories festooned with bats, skulls, or coffins, then you probably should go turn in your Goth card (which doesn't exist) right now. So feel free to gently tease them about their oh-so-dark lives and fashion choices. (The Lady of the Manners once worked for a manager who would preface the news of impending overtime with, "You're saving up for a new pair of pointy boots, right? Well, have I got news for you!") Just keep in mind that if your gothy acquaintance asks you to drop it or stop, the correct response is, "Okay, I'm sorry," not "It's just a joke! Don't you have a sense of humor?"

Speaking of senses of humor, try not to be shocked by the sometimes morbid sense of humor that most Goths display. Jokes about crawling back to their coffins, hiding the bodies, being nocturnal, obeying the voices in their heads, or being willing to work extra hours so they can avoid the angry yellow burny thing in the sky are just that: jokes. Spookier-than-thou, black-hearted jokes, maybe, but certainly nothing to worry about.

The key here is to treat everyone, Goths included, the way you would like to be treated. Just because some people look different from you or cherish different things, doesn't mean they are exempt from being treated courteously. This may come as a surprise to some people, but most Goths don't spend time thinking of ways to annoy or freak out other people. It's true! The Lady of the Manners is well aware that most of us secretly believe we are at the center of the universe and that anything someone else says or does is loaded with subtext meant for us alone. Which is, when you stop to think about it, utter twaddle. And you the reader may be sitting there thinking, "But I don't believe that!" to which the Lady of the Manners would raise an eyebrow and gently ask whether you're being completely truthful. There's nothing wrong with indulging in a tiny bit of solipsism and narcissism; you just need to make sure to treat other people kindly and politely.

If a Goth is inexplicably mean to me in the Hot Topic where I get my hair dye, can I name-check you and threaten to file a report? (Oh, how the Lady of the Manners wishes that would work!)

The Lady of the Manners is sad to say she's heard of this sort of thing far more often than she'd like. Someone who is not obviously part of the Goth subculture receives poor treatment at a traditionally Goth-oriented venue. For every Goth who complains of suffering rude and insensitive treatment, there is a non-Goth who has innocently wandered into a Hot Topic or other store that caters to "alternative" types and been sneered at. This, obviously, is not acceptable. But why does it happen?

For one thing, Goths—especially the younger members of the subculture—can be a bit, erm, insular. Cliquish. Wary of outsiders and *very* wary of "normal" people trying to appropriate their style or subcultural signifiers. So when someone they don't auto-matically recognize as "one of us" turns up buying purple hair dye or stripy tights, they get defensive and snippy. Again, this behavior is displayed primarily by the younger members of the Goth sub-culture. They're usually so wrapped up in defining themselves as spooky and different, as Real Goths, that they have a knee-jerk reac-tion to people they don't define as Real Goths doing "Goth" things. (The Lady of the Manners suspects that younger Goths react this way in part because they are constantly being told that their fas-cination with the darker side of life is a phase they'll grow out of, and that when they grow up, they'll feel differently about the whole thing. This, quite naturally, annoys the younger Goths and makes them defensive about what they consider to be theirs. Also, many babybats have had to put up with taunts and abuse from their more "normal" peers and classmates, which makes them wary when someone who doesn't look like them starts shopping around for skull jewelry and dark lipstick.)

Then there's that whole "costume" thing that the Lady of the Manners mentioned earlier. The Lady of the Manners is all for everyone playing with black-hued finery, but even she gets a bit cranky every October when people accost her in stores demand-ing to know where she got her costume, and whether she can help them find one like it. "Oh, it's not a costume," she patiently informs them. "I dress like this every day." Depending on where she is and how busy she might be, the Lady of the Manners will sometimes offer suggestions to the costume-seekers as to where they might find gothy bits and trinkets, but usually she just continues on with whatever she was doing.

So if a Goth is mean or rude to you, what should you do? Can you name-check the Lady of the Manners and prompt an apology from the black-clad crankypants? The Lady of the Manners is sad to say that almost certainly wouldn't work. (Her plans for global domination of the Goth subculture haven't come to fruition just yet, you see.) No, what you should do is . . . ignore the offending party. Ignore the rude behavior or, at the most, mildly point out the rudeness but don't get into any sort of argument about it. In other words, react just as you would to anyone who treated you rudely.

That is how you would treat other rude people, isn't it? You wouldn't be even ruder in return, initiating an ever-escalating war of bad behavior, would you? Forgive the Lady of the Manners for seeking to reassure herself, but she's seen some dreadful examples of that sort of thing. If you're feeling especially chipper and cheeky, you could try gently

reminding the gothy type that, "The nice lady from Gothic Charm School always says that Goths should try to be polite," but be warned that the gothy type in question may very well just roll her eyes at you.

A few words for the Goths reading this chapter

Look, the Lady of the Manners doesn't care how affronted your delicate spooky sensibilities are by the sight of people who obviously aren't Goths buying Goth goodies. So what? Maybe they're buying a present for a friend or relative. Maybe they've decided they finally want to explore the Goth subculture. Or maybe they *are* purchasing hair dye and a shirt with a bat on it for a costume. So what? There is no Secret Goth cabal that must give its stamp of approval before someone is allowed to purchase skull jewelry and stripy tights, and getting cranky about it is more than a little ridiculous. Some of you may remember a stereotype about Goths from years ago (the Lady of the Manners hasn't heard it thrown about quite as much recently but is sure that its shadow still lingers over the subculture): Goths are all stuck-up, snobby, elitist twerps who are full of themselves and don't like anyone. Does that ring any bells? The Lady of the Manners suspects that stereotype was born out of a Goth defense mechanism: stave off taunts and harassment by acting as if you don't like anyone. This strategy, while effective, just invites other sorts of problems. Now, the Lady of the Manners doesn't presume to speak for everyone else in the Goth subculture (again, while the Lady of the Manners does cherish some frivolous notions of gothy global domination, she's still working out some flaws in her plans), but she is awfully tired of the "Goths are all stuck-up and bitchy drama queens" stereotype. Really, that pose just helps reinforce the notion that Goth is a crabby teen phase everyone grows out of eventually. The Lady of the Manners is of the belief that being polite to people, whether or not they share your interests, is far more shocking than being surly and arrogant. For whatever reason, people just don't expect black-clad spooksters to be polite; when we are, they're frequently flabbergasted and so taken aback they seem to forget whatever prejudices they may have been harboring.

The Lady of the Manners is not saying that if everyone was polite to each other the universe would be a perfect place full of rainbows and harmony and happy vampires. But you must admit, everyday life would be a lot more pleasant.

THREE

Babygoths

How to show support to your babygoth or babybat without relinquishing the keys to the hearse, and everything you need to know to Not Freak Out

Now that the Lady of the Manners has put you at ease about some of the more pervasive rumors concerning Goths (she has, hasn't she?), you may still be wondering about what you should do if you have a Goth in your family. What if your child seems to be exploring the dark side?

When the Lady of the Manners was a little girl, she announced to her parents that she was going to be the Wicked Witch of the West when she grew up. The Lady of the Manners's parents smiled at her and said, "That's nice, dear." When the Lady of the Manners was a little bit older and allowed to roam freely through the local library, she would trundle home laden with books about witches, vampires, and ghosts. When the concerned librarian pointed this out to the Lady of the Manners's parents, they smiled and said, "Isn't it wonderful how much she likes to read?" When the Lady of the Manners hit adolescence and started doodling on her face with eyeliner and listening to strange music, the Lady of the Manners's parents said, "That's very creative, dear. If you get straight A's on your next report card, you can dye your hair purple." What the Lady of the Manners is trying to show by example here is that becoming a Goth doesn't mean becoming a Satanist, doing drugs, joining a cult, or contemplating suicide, or murder. But many people (most of whom should know better) will assume exactly those sorts of things about your fledgling Goth child based solely on his or her appearance. If you really want to be supportive, speak up in your child's defense. If someone makes a comment about the way your child looks, talk about how glad you are that he is an individual with his own sense of style. Explain that just because your child chooses to look "that way" doesn't make him evil or disturbed. And it certainly *doesn't* make you a bad parent.

Be warned: even people close to you might spout off with this sort of nonsense. Practice your best calm, polite tone of voice coupled with an icy smile. Better yet, teach your babygoth to respond to these comments in a polite, "Yes, I always look like this; no it's not a costume; you're right, it isn't Halloween yet" manner. Because the truth is, no matter what your child looks like, there will always be people who make snide comments or say hurtful things. The earlier you can teach your children how to deal with conflict gracefully, the better off they'll be when dealing with all sorts of things throughout their lives.

Nowadays, there are all sorts of places where one can buy what amounts to a "Goth starter kit." Shopping malls are filled with chain stores that cater to the young and spooky. There's nothing wrong with that, and everyone needs to start somewhere. However, not only can that get expensive, but it's rather . . . stale. Not creative. Even (gasp!) a touch conformist, in that "I am a unique dark snowflake, just like everyone else" sort of way. Instead, encourage your child to develop a personal style by visiting thrift stores together and assembling a unique gothy wardrobe. Not only will you save money, but the skills your child will learn from this (such as sewing, painting, developing a sense of design) are useful things everyone should know. If your child's interest in DIY fashion becomes strong enough, perhaps you would allow her to host gothy craft days. Let her invite her spookster friends over for an afternoon of working on craft projects or trying out new looks with each other's wardrobes and makeup. (See Chapter 8 for a whole flock of suggestions about customizing basic items of clothing.) If the notion of a house full of babybats playing with eyeliner makes you wince, remember that you don't have to be right there sewing on lace trim or helping apply liquid eyeliner. Being willing to let your babybat's friends come hang out in your home without expressing overt disapproval will mean a lot to them. Besides, this way you and the other parents can feel reassured knowing the flock of babybats are safe at home instead of roaming off to the mall and loitering for hours on end.

Another thing to remember about fledgling Goths: You're still the parent! You are perfectly within your rights to say things like, "I don't think you should wear a corset to school," "Please don't wear black lipstick when we go to your grandparents' house," or "That's inappropriately revealing for someone your age; please go change clothes." If you wouldn't tolerate certain types of behavior before, there's no reason for you to go along with them now, just because your child has developed an interest in Goth. (The Lady of the Manners is well aware that this will be read with dismay by some of her teenage readers, but she hopes they understand that some things just aren't appropriate when you're a young gothling. Besides, compromising with your parents on some things will go a long way toward keeping the family peace, and there will be pages and pages of advice for you later on in the book. Patience, young Snarklings. Your time will come.)

Try to keep an open mind about things, and do some research. Don't dismiss something out of hand because the only information you have about your child's newfound spookiness comes from sensationalist news stories designed to boost TV ratings. Ask your child questions and take the opportunity to discuss his interests as impartially as possible. Those new interests may be things you wouldn't have chosen for him, but it doesn't make the interests themselves awful or evil.

And for heaven's sake, don't refer to your child's interest in Goth as "a phase." Maybe it is, maybe it isn't, but calling it a phase is a quick way to convince her that you don't take her seriously. Even if it is a phase, there's nothing wrong with that. Everyone has phases of exploration, be they football, musical instruments, or black eyeliner. Trying on new identities isn't a cause for alarm. But one thing you should attempt to avoid is trying *too* hard to share your babygoth's every new enthusiasm. Being supportive is one thing; rushing out and buying yourself a matching black velvet outfit and tagging along everywhere is another. Being a supportive parent is good; a smothering "we can do everything together!" approach is not. Even if you think you and your child are best friends, there are going to be times when she thinks that you're horrible, that you are evil personified, and that you just don't understand her! The Lady of the Manners is blessed with absolutely wonderful parents, and there were times when all she did was lock herself in her room and sulk because she was convinced they didn't understand her. (The Lady of the Manners has been known to call up her parents and apologize for her adolescent self; the Lady of the Manners's parents are vastly amused by this.)

The moody, sullen, brooding aspects of teenage Gothdom are going to happen no matter what you do. Chances are, they would have set in even if your child wasn't a Goth; isn't sullenness and brooding a part of adolescence for everyone? You should still make sure your kid's okay, but don't assume that things are worse than they really are just because of some black velvet and a lot of eyeliner. These things are not necessarily cries for help. Perhaps your kid has discovered a form of self-expression, and that's a good thing.

Babybat-friendly books the Lady of the Manners recommends:

- *The Vampire Kisses* series by Ellen Schreiber
- *A Series of Unfortunate Events* by Lemony Snicket
- *The Scary Godmother* storybooks by Jill Thompson
- *Coraline* by Neil Gaiman
- *The Wolves of Willoughby Chase* by Joan Aiken
- *The Spiderwick Chronicles* by Holly Black
- *The Witches* by Roald Dahl
- *The Dark Is Rising* series (*The Dark Is Rising, Greenwitch, The Grey King,* and *Silver on the Tree*) by Susan Cooper
- *Bizenghast* by M. Alice LeGrow (manga)
- *The Wee Free Men, A Hat Full of Sky,* and *Wintersmith* by Terry Pratchett

What else can you do?

Use participation in the Goth subculture as a reward for good grades or behavior you'd like to see more of: your child can do "x" thing if he meets a certain goal. For example, you might allow your son to color his hair an unnatural shade as a reward for good grades or buy your daughter a coveted item of clothing for helping out around the house. The Lady of the Manners's very own parents used these tactics when she was a moody black-clad teen. And they worked very well.

Encourage your child to explore the literary and artistic roots of the Gothic movement. Don't assume those explorations should stop at the roots of the Gothic movement either. Help your babybat seek out the modern flourishes of Gothic literature and art. While many parents (and other adults) narrow their eyes suspiciously at comics and manga, there are many gothy *and* kid-friendly titles to be found on those shelves.

Encourage your child in any creative projects she may start. Many an introspective babybat's dabbling in writing, photography, or illustration has helped her decide what she wants to do when she grows up. Hours spent on the computer creating desktop backgrounds, user icons, and websites teach useful skills kids can someday use to find themselves a "real job," even if all of their effort and tech skills seem to be focused on creating fan sites for whatever band or book has captured their hearts. Even seemingly eccentric creative pursuits such as making etchings of gravestones or making toy monsters can turn into more than "just" hobbies.

Talk to your kid and find out what has drawn her to the Goth subculture in the first place, and you might just discover what she is passionate about. But above all, remember that having a child who is a Goth isn't a bad thing. After all, the Lady of the Manners's parents think she turned out just fine.

What if my children hide behind me wide-eyed?

What if you aren't raising a fledgling Goth but keep seeing gothy types while you're out and about with your family? Before you start worrying that a black-clad person is deliberately trying to scare your children, keep in mind that many children are shy or nervous about anyone they don't know, no matter what the stranger looks like. Just because your child is hiding behind you with wide eyes doesn't mean that the person he's hiding from is scary or bad. On the other hand, should you coax your child into talking to this person? No, not necessarily. In the Lady of the Manners's mind, trying to coax small children out of their shells to interact with strangers they've randomly met doesn't seem terribly productive or useful.

But! Don't add to your child's nervousness. Don't act like Goths are a terrible danger to be avoided, and especially don't point or make rude comments. Children imitate the people closest to them, even when they perhaps shouldn't. Once, while on a very full flight home from a trip, the Lady of the Manners was seated next to a young girl. The girl, fascinated by the Lady of the Manners's frilly skirts, striped tights, and velvet jacket, spent the flight cheerfully chattering away at the Lady of the Manners about her older sister, what books she liked, her opinions of the in-flight movies, and anything else that crossed her mind. When the girl asked the Lady of the Manners about her outfit, the Lady of the Manners explained that she was a Goth. At which point the girl's eyes became very wide, and she shrank back in her seat a little bit.

"My stepdad says Goths are scary," confided the young lady.

"Hmmm. Really?" asked the Lady of the Manners. "Do you think I'm scary?"

"No. You're really nice!" was the immediate response.

"See? Goths aren't scary. Just like most people aren't scary. Why does your stepdad say Goths are scary?"

What followed was a recitation of all the stereotypes the Lady of the Manners had expected to hear. Goths look weird. They're different, and being different is bad. They're creepy, dangerous, violent. As the girl rattled off the ideas her stepfather had tried to indoctrinate her with, the Lady of the Manners purposefully didn't get angry or upset and worked very hard at keeping her facial expression neutral. Once the girl was done with her litany of prejudices, she looked at the Lady of the Manners and made a skeptical face.

"But you're really nice!" she repeated. "Why would my stepdad say stuff like that?"

"Maybe because he doesn't know any Goths?" the Lady of the Manners offered.

"Well, that's dumb. I'm going to tell him about you and how nice you are. Maybe he'll stop being scared of Goths."

"That would be nice."

And with that decided, the young girl went back to asking the Lady of the Manners for help solving some of the puzzles in the "young wizard" activity book with which she had been amusing herself.

Filling children's heads with vague fears of people you don't know much about seems, in the Lady of the Manners's opinion, to be a disservice. It's a big world, full of strange and unexpected people and things. Just because you don't know much about something (be it a foreign culture or a subculture) doesn't make it wrong or bad, and teaching your children that sort of thinking can only limit them. Teaching children to be automatically suspicious of anyone who appears different can rob them of chances for understanding and growth. Kids shouldn't assume everyone they meet will be friendly and harmless, but neither should they be afraid of people who dress or speak differently than they do.

A few words for the Goths reading this section

Yes, it's annoying when you're wandering along, minding your own business, and someone makes a big deal about her children being scared by you. Especially if it's apparent that the children aren't just being shy kids but have been indoctrinated with the notion that people who look different are to be regarded with fear and disdain. Unless you're in a situation like the one the Lady of the Manners was in on the plane, there's not a lot you can do about it. Other than, of course, being as polite as possible and not sneering, exaggerating your potentially scary nature, or getting into any sort of argument with the parent about her seemingly closed-minded worldview. No, just perhaps wave at the kidlings and go on with whatever it was you were doing before.

What if my children run toward them shrieking with glee?

Children, in the Lady of the Manners's experience, are drawn to Goths like bees to flowers (or moths to moonflowers, as it were). This should come as no surprise, if you stop and think about it. Goths tend to be people of high visual contrast: all black and white with accents of vivid jewel tones (or pink, in the Lady of the Manners's case). The same sort of visual principles on which most cartoons are, as a matter of fact. Most Goths look like they're from another, more exciting world. So of course children are attracted to that.

Does that mean you should let your children scamper up to the first Goth they see? Well, no. No more than you should let your children gleefully run toward anyone that you, and they, don't know. But don't assume that the eccentric-looking person with the outrageous hair or clothing is a danger to them either. If your child points out a Goth with excitement or interest, don't feel you have to warn him or her to watch out for the Goth. Most Goths, when a small child exclaims over the way they look or waves at them, think such behavior is cute and will smile or wave back.

However, don't fall into the trap of thinking that because someone looks like he just escaped from the set of a particularly wacky movie, he would be delighted to spend time entertaining your offspring. Goths are not zany costumed characters or entertainers. Actually, now that the Lady of the Manners stops to think on it, some of them very well might be, but probably not the sort who specialize in children's entertainment. Even if they were, unless you've hired them for a special event, you shouldn't assume that they will stop whatever they are doing and amuse your children at length. Again, it comes down to treating that eccentric person in black clothing in the same way you'd treat anyone else. Asking questions of that eccentric person in black is just fine. Letting your children grab at her, or using her as a distraction for your children while you go off and do something else, is most assuredly not.

You may think the Lady of the Manners is being a touch dramatic about the whole "do not assume the Goths will entertain your children" point. Oh, Snarklings, she's not. The Lady of the Manners will freely admit that her preferred wardrobe makes her look like she's escaped from a touring production of *Mary Poppins* as visualized by Tim Burton, which may give some people the idea that she's just like a lovable and magical nanny and thus is willing to child-wrangle at the drop of a veiled hat. While the Lady of the Manners is many things, a magical nanny she is not. The same goes for other Goths, many of whom have talked at great length with the Lady of the Manners about this same phenomenon. The Lady of the Manners suspects this happens more frequently to those of us who have a more Victorian and/or whimsical style than it might to the Goths who favor a deathrock and/or Grrr! Stompy! look, but regardless of what corner of the subcultural closet a Goth is exploring, there always seems to be someone who assumes this Goth will be offering a free show and babysitting service.

A few words for the Goths
reading this section

The Lady of the Manners begs you, no matter what your feelings toward children are, to be as polite as you possibly can manage toward them. Yes, even if their parents are looking at you like you've just appeared in a black cloud of sulfurous smoke and are about to stride forth to destroy everything they hold dear. Yes, even if you really don't like children. Please don't give in to any urges to scare kids or their parents, no matter what provocation may be offered. Why? Because, like it or not, the majority of the mainstream population is already a little unnerved by us spooky types. One of the least helpful things a Goth can do is strengthen that uneasy feeling and make "normal people" even more wary of us. Does that mean you should try to make friends with all the little kids you meet, let them clamber all over you, and be oh so zany and fun for their amusement? Bah. Of course not. The Lady of the Manners likes children (in general and is very fond of some specific ones) but is not willing to be extremely friendly and approachable to every munchkin she meets. So remember to politely answer any questions from children you meet. Don't tell them stories about how you're a vampire or that you're going to eat them or give them to the monsters. (Unless, of course, the children in question are close to you and have been raised on jolly stories of friendly monsters, just like the Lady of the Manners's assorted godchildren have been.) However, in all seriousness, do not try to scare the kids or parents. Please.

How do I explain Goth to my children if they ask me about it?

Children, being curious and inquisitive creatures, will, of course, ask you about these strange and flamboyant people they've just en-

countered. Why do they look like that? What do they do? The Lady of the Manners isn't going to tell you how much of an explanation to give to your children; that depends on how old they are and how much information you think they might be able to absorb. But some points of reference for ease of explanation are as follows:

- **Halloween.** Goths love Halloween, as do most children. The dressing up, bats, jack-o'-lanterns, skeletons, and ghosts, the once-a-year celebration of spooky things that most people usually find creepy—these are some of the aspects of Halloween that Goths and children hold equally dear, along with the hope that there is more to this world than is readily apparent, that whimsy and magic are to be found everywhere. Children seem to have an understanding of the magic of Halloween all the way down to their very bones; not magic as in casting spells, but magic as in the sense that anything can happen, that anything can be equal parts spine-tingling and marvelous. Goths are people who haven't lost that childlike sense of wonder, who look for spine-tingling and spooky thrills on more than just one day of the year.

- **Fairy tales.** Fairy tales are, in some ways, the *original* Gothic stories. They're full of symbols and archetypes that helped mold the Goth subculture. (While the Lady of the Manners isn't referencing the twinkly, pastel, Disney-fied versions of fairy tales, she knows that many a fledgling babybat was mesmerized by Maleficent from *Sleeping Beauty* or stared longingly at the magnificent library from *Beauty and the Beast*.) Eerie witches, spooky forests, ghosts of both helpful and dangerous natures, horrible beasts masquerading as people (and people disguised or enchanted to appear as hideous beasts)—all of these not only demonstrate that everything is not always what it seems, but also that it could be mysterious and exciting. To be a Goth is to yearn, even if just the tiniest bit, for the everyday humdrum world to change into something slightly out of the ordinary. It's not that Goths want to ignore or run away from the real world, it's just that we wish, we demand, that there may be more to the real world than what so many other people are willing to settle for. Children can easily understand that mindset: every forest (or even every city sewer or subway tunnel) could be home to strange creatures, and there could be monsters hiding under the bed. Those strange creatures or monsters could mean you harm, or they could be seeking your help with a magical quest. Either way, doesn't that sound more interesting than doing your homework and going to bed on time?

The Addams Family and the work of Tim Burton. While there are Goths out there who dislike both *The Addams Family* and everything Tim Burton has done, they are in the minority of the subculture. Both of these examples have a quirky, slightly off-center view of the world and are populated with larger-than-life eccentric characters, characters who don't impose their views or philosophies on anyone else but just want to live their lives in the way that makes them happy. Not to mention the strong sense of whimsy that both *The Addams Family* and most Tim Burton movies embody. A severed hand as a household pet seems unremarkable in the context of the Addams household, and of course there's a whole land of monsters that dedicate their lives to creating Halloween. Why wouldn't there be? Again, for some reason the "mainstream" world seems to think that a sense of whimsy and fantasy are teenage phases to grow out of. Most Goths don't agree with that way of thinking at all. Plus there's the strong, immediately recognizable visual styles of both examples. Everyone seems to know what Wednesday Addams's and Morticia's dresses look like, and the "Tim Burton-influenced" label is slapped on seemingly anything with black and white stripy accents and wrought-iron curlicues. Those strong visual styles resonate with kids, who are drawn to anything cartoonish and otherworldly.

Goth parents and raising the next generation of babybats

Do you have to turn in your Goth card when you become a parent? Is being a Goth only suitable for those who never have to think about diaper bags and babysitters? Oh, don't be silly.

The Lady of the Manners can see where this sort of confusion or worry springs from. To many people (including those who are part of the spookily clad masses), being a Goth involves a regular schedule of nightclubbing, parties, and a wildly impractical taste in clothing. If that is all being a Goth means, then of course it seems as if being a Goth is incompatible with being a parent.

However, for the majority of the spooky creatures of the night, being a Goth means more than just clubs, parties, and eccentric clothing. (Though the Lady of the Manners is fond of all those things and is rather infamously devoted to the "eccentric clothing" part.) Being a Goth means that you have an appreciation for the beauty that can be found in darkness or decay, that you have a healthy sense of the absurd, an appreciation for whimsy, and are not afraid to be your own person. In the Lady of the Manners's eyes, those also seem like very good qualities for a parent to have.

Of course, becoming a parent does require some changes to

your spooky lifestyle. Going out to Goth Night at the local club can't be quite as spur of the moment as it once might have been, what with arranging for babysitters and such. Not to mention, as the Lady of the Manners has learned from friends who are parents, wrangling babybats is tiring, to put it mildly. Some days, finding the energy to do more than flop on the couch and stare into space is an insurmountable obstacle. Does that mean you need to wave good-bye to your social life? Don't be silly. It just means that you'll be going out less frequently and your social life will probably shift to more evenings at home with friends.

Then there's the question of wardrobe: excessive ruffles, frills, and opulent fabrics don't mix well with day-to-day parental life. (The Lady of the Manners can see where PVC clothing provides ease of cleanup with most messes, but the Lady of the Manners is also fairly certain that most garments made from that fabric are not an ideal style for most parents.) Does that mean you need to give up your wardrobe of gloom? Of course not. It just means that you will need to keep "is it washable?" firmly in mind while clothes shopping. (A helpful hint: almost all stretch velvet *is* safe to throw in the washer and dryer, as long as you stick to lower-temperature settings. If the label says "poly/spandex," you *should* be able to ignore that pesky Dry Clean Only tag. But be wary of anything with beading, appliqués, or delicate embroidery. In other words, if the garment is particularly important to you, you probably don't want to wear it while feeding, changing, or doing anything else with your babybat that has the potential for messy accidents.)

The Lady of the Manners is strongly in favor of Goths becoming parents. In fact, the only concern the Lady of the Manners has about Goths being parents is that some may try a little too hard to turn their children into perfect little clones of Wednesday and Pugsley Addams. It's all well and good to dress them in clothes that say "babybat" and give them fuzzy toy monsters to hug, but don't feel betrayed if they like Disney cartoons and sports too. Remember that children are separate people with their own (frequently strongly expressed) likes and dislikes.

Something that all Goth parents still need to watch out for is other people's hostility and disapproval. Sadly, many misguided people out there think Goths are not fit to be parents, an opinion the Lady of the Manners feels is utter nonsense, of course. But that doesn't stop interfering busybodies from glaring accusingly (or worse!) at Goth parents. Ignore those types whenever possible (but ignore them with a polite smile!) and instead concentrate on raising your babybats to be happy, well-adjusted, and possibly (hopefully) spooky.

What about those of you, like the Lady of the Manners, who aren't parents but whose friends are? Firstly, don't assume that having children caused your friends to lose all interest in everything else. Most parents are eager for (if not desperately craving!) conversation with people about something other than their children. Just be aware that no matter how fascinating that conversation may be, it will get interrupted at times by the necessities of child rearing. That's just how things are, and getting annoyed or frustrated with your friends or the children is ridiculous. If you are one of those people who Just Doesn't Like Children (and there's no shame in admitting this), then you need to accept that you probably won't see your friends as often as you once might have. Just be honest with yourself *and* your friends about your feelings, and try not to be antagonistic about the subject when it comes up. However, if you're one of those people who does like children, then why not offer to babysit occasionally? Even the most devoted parents cherish a night away from their spooky bundles of joy and would probably be delighted to give their babybats a chance to spend more time around their extended (Addams) family. If it takes a village to raise a child, there is nothing that says the village can't be decorated with a motif of friendly bats and crushed velvet.

FOUR

Help! I'm a Goth and My Parent/Friend/Significant Other/Coworker Doesn't Understand Me!

How to reassure people you aren't a Satanist, drug fiend, or psycho killer

Let's face it, Snarklings: Goth doesn't exactly have the world's best image and, really, it never will. A subculture with a core philosophy of finding and appreciating beauty in unexpected and sometimes very dark places, that takes the majority of its aesthetic cues from horror movies, funereal attire, and other morbid things, is never going to become something that doesn't raise any eyebrows. Which, really, is just fine and the way that it should be, but sometimes the Lady of the Manners wishes that the general public's reaction to our spooky and black-clad selves wasn't always quite so . . . alarmed.

But because most non-Goths tend to be at the very least a little disconcerted by Goths, we have to deal with the misconceptions.

The Lady of the Manners won't lie to you: dealing with those misconceptions can be tedious and annoying. Yes, even the Lady of the Manners sometimes feels the temptation to give someone her very best menacing smile and "Why yes, I *am* contemplating what your blood might taste like" stare when she's regarded with unease and apprehension by strangers. But she doesn't succumb to that temptation, because no matter how amusing it may seem, this reaction is counterproductive and only confirms everyone's worst suspicions about Goths.

So how should you reassure people that you're not contemplating scary acts of occult-tinged violence just because you're wearing all black? By being polite and pleasant to people when they ask you questions about your appearance, no matter how dubious they may seem of your reaction, of course. But what if the people you need to reassure are not random strangers but people close to you, like friends or family?

First things first: ask them what they think Goth means and try not to roll your eyes or snort derisively at whatever sensational movie-of-the-week nonsense they come up with. Instead, after they're done talking about the dangers of Goth, gently explain what Goth *really* is. Start with "family-friendly" examples such as *The Addams Family*, *The Munsters*, and Tim Burton movies such as *Beetlejuice*, *The Nightmare Before Christmas*, or *Corpse Bride*. Talk about Gothic literature, how the Gothic movement has been around, in one form or another, for hundreds of years, and that "gloomy and decadent" does not automatically equal "death-obsessed and dangerous."

The next thing to do is talk about why *you're* attracted to the Goth subculture. What about it resonates with you and makes you happy? This can be a bit tricky, especially if you haven't really thought about it yourself; while "Because it's cool!" and "Because I like it!" are perfectly valid reasons, they aren't going to go very far in helping someone else understand your point of view.

(An important aside to the younger Goths reading this: telling your parents you are a Goth because "wearing black on the outside matches how I feel inside," while perhaps true, will not reassure them in the slightest. Neither will telling them that you like freaking people out or that your friends are doing it too. You need to come up with some other, less troubling things to say, kiddos.)

The most important ideas to get across to whomever you're trying to reassure is that Goth isn't a cult and that being interested in Goth doesn't mean you're going to hurt yourself or anyone else. As the Lady of the Manners has pointed out in previous chapters, being a Goth is no more dangerous than being a fan of sports, video games, knitting, or NASCAR; we Goths just look a bit more eccentric than other people. (Only a *bit* more eccentric, when you stop to really think about it, because some of the outfits and costumes sports fans put together to show their support are *astonishing*. Face paint and tinsel wigs in team colors are some of the milder examples of fan adornment the Lady of the Manners has seen.)

Be warned: no matter how eloquently you explain Goth and what it means to you, the people you love may still not get it. The Lady of the Manners is especially sad to say this is more likely to happen to some of the younger Goths. Your parents may dismiss the whole thing as a silly and/or troubling phase. If this happens there's, sadly, not really much you can do. Whenever the topic of your gothness comes up, keep your temper as much as possible and try to avoid doing anything that you know will anger your parents. (For example, don't dye your hair shocking pink if you know they don't want you to drastically alter your

79

Help! I'm a Goth and My Parent/Friend/Significant Other/Coworker Doesn't Understand Me!

appearance.) The Lady of the Manners is not telling you to give up being a Goth—not in the slightest! Just be aware that you may not be able to express as much of your spooky nature as you want at this time. Be patient, and just keep trying to explain to your family that wearing black clothes and heavy eye makeup doesn't mean you've turned into a horrible and scary creature.

Helpful tips for convincing your parents to let you express yourself through your clothing (but don't kid yourself: the Lady of the Manners wouldn't let you wear a corset to school either)

"You are not leaving the house dressed like that." All Goths have heard these words at one time or another in their lives, probably during their school years. For every babybat whose parent accepts her and says, "Sure, you can put red streaks in your hair," there are oodles of other gothlings who have to plead and bargain for every scrap of spooky darkness they want to include in their clothing. Whyyyyyyyyy are your parents being so unreasonable about your turning to the dark side when you are just trying to express yourself? Maybe your parents have fallen prey to the assorted misconceptions about Goth that the media likes to keep yammering on about. Maybe it's because your

parents are worried that you'll be picked on and bullied if you look different from everyone else. Perhaps it's because your parents are a tiny bit worried that people will judge them to be bad parents if you're running around with black clothes, blue hair, and heavy makeup. (The Lady of the Manners is willing to bet at least two frilly black parasols that most parental concerns are a mixture of all of the above reasons.)

Yes, Snarklings, the Lady of the Manners discourages you from stocking your wardrobe of gloom with items found at retail chains in shopping malls. It is never too early to start assembling your own take on Gothic fashion, and creating your own style is easier when you're not wearing the same long black coat with straps and chains as every other black-clad and possibly sullen teen.

So is there anything you can do in order to reassure your silly, worried parents that it's perfectly okay for you to wear black clothes? Of course there is, and the Lady of the Manners isn't even talking about the really obvious tactics. (The really obvious tactics: do as well as you possibly can in school, do your chores around the house without whining, and try to be as much of a model "good kid" as possible. The less your parents have to complain about with regard to your general behavior, the stronger your case for permission to dress in a manner that is pleasing to you will be.)

What are the non-obvious things you can do to help your parents see that a spooky wardrobe does not equal a troubled teen?

 Learn to sew, and show your parents that by making your own gothy clothing *and* accessories, you're expressing your creativity *and* learning very useful skills. Now, the Lady of the Manners doesn't mean that you should set out to handcraft everything you might ever want to wear; for one thing, the

Lady of the Manners suspects that you don't have that much free time, what with school and family life and whatnot. But parents (generally) love the notion of their kids learning practical skills, which might make them a bit more willing to sigh and accept the blacker-than-black color scheme (with some stripy accents) you have adopted.

🦇 Point out that a lot of the clothing you long for can be created from garments found at thrift stores. When the Lady of the Manners was a spooky alterna-teen, her parents were delighted that she wanted to shop for her back-to-school wardrobe at the local thrift stores. Show your parents that your Goth aesthetic will save the family budget the expense of trendy mainstream fashion.

🦇 Show your parents Goth clothes that don't look like club wear or send a sexualized message. Which is why, Snarklings, the Lady of the Manners wouldn't let you wear a corset to school either. (Well, all right, if you wore the corset over a shirt that covered you from neck to waist with a nice skirt that was not a micro-mini, then the Lady of the Manners probably would let you wear a corset to school.) Yes, corsets and stockings and fishnet shirts and vinyl trousers are all interesting items of clothing; however, they all have a subtext of sexuality to them. Vinyl clothes project "S&M! Kinky weirdoes!" to many people, while corsets, stockings, and fishnet or lace clothing display one's attributes in a rather noticeable manner. While the Lady of the Manners thinks there is absolutely nothing wrong with any of those garments, she feels there is a time and a place for them and school isn't it.

You see, your parents probably worry that you might attract the wrong sort of attention, the sort of attention that makes them uncomfortable. Thanks to the mainstream media, many people assume that someone in Goth regalia is some sort of creepy, deviant freak, which is not how parents want to think about their baby.

While your more "normal" classmates can probably get away with wearing skin-tight jeans or extremely low-cut tank tops without people making assumptions about them, Goths need to be a bit more aware of the message their outfits might send. Opting for some modesty in your shadowy clothing choices will probably go a long way toward addressing your parents' concerns. (For a more in-depth look at dress codes, both spoken and implied, scamper ahead to Chapter 8.)

Goths and school (and why these aren't necessarily the best years of your life)

The notion that your teen years are the "best years of your life," that you've reached the pinnacle of your existence and everything after will be pointless tedium, is a terrifying one, isn't it? The Lady of the Manners is here to tell you, Snarklings, that this particular common statement is dead wrong. Nobody, and the Lady of the Manners means nobody, has a completely wonderful time throughout adolescence. Sure, there are some bright spots, but for the most part, one's teenage years are character-forming in the sense that if you can survive them, you'll have a greater understanding of human misery and angst. Why do you think all the John Hughes movies of the '80s about misfit teens were so popular? Because they struck a chord in just about everyone who ever saw them. Also, after most people grow up a bit, they find it charming when someone admits that his or her high school years were a trial. (In fact, the Lady of the Manners has heard the phrase, "I bet you were one of those popular people in high school," used as a scornful insult a handful of times.)

However, because you are a Goth, you may experience more than your fair share of school annoyances. Most teenagers naturally seem to fall into a pack mentality and tend to react poorly to others who reject the herd. No, it's not fair or right, but it happens. Does this mean you should hide your interest in Goth or that you should work on blending in with the rest of the kids at your school? Good heavens, not even a little bit. Instead, work on developing a healthy amount of self-confidence and realize that the quality of your life does not depend upon whether everyone likes you. Self-confidence is one of the most important safeguards against the casual torture school can bring. Teens seem to have an unerring knack for finding and exploiting the emotional weak spots of their classmates, especially if those weak spots involve wanting others to like or approve of you. The Lady of the Man-

ners agrees that it is very nice to be liked and not to be mocked or teased, but you know what, Snarklings? Try very hard not to let your self-esteem rest on whether or not your fellow students like or approve of you. If they don't, they *don't*, and there's not really a lot you can do to change their minds. So don't spend your school years tormenting yourself just because someone thinks you're weird.

Learn to cultivate a quietly superior attitude as your armor at school. If or when classmates start harassing you, smile at them in a faintly amused, faintly elitist manner, and then walk away. Don't get into name-calling fights (or any other type!) because you won't win them. It doesn't matter if you're right and they're wrong; the other kids won't be willing to admit it. If you can just act quietly indifferent to them and not react to their taunts and attempts to annoy you, they will eventually get bored and find a new person to bother. Many people who indulge in bullying behavior are looking for a reaction, any reaction. If you don't give them that reaction, they'll often leave you alone. Not always, but more often than not.

Another plus to the advice above is that authority figures (be they parents, teachers, or something else) tend to be impressed by good manners, even if they think you're a freak. The Lady of the Manners survived a lot of slings and arrows in high school (and even in college and the "grown-up" world of employment) by being mannerly and polite. In a condescending and somewhat self-confident manner, sometimes, it is true, but most of the people attempting to torment her didn't catch on to that aspect. (Of course, that is not a good reason to brush up on one's manners, but it gives the task a devilish and sneaky sense of fun.)

However, if the fight escalates, *walk away*. Find some sort of nominal adult presence as soon as possible. Most tormentors won't continue with their "fun" if there is a grown-up around to witness it. If the people persecuting you don't stop once you move to such a location, it's even more important to resist responding in a similar manner. Try to get the adult in the area involved. (As wrong as it is, most adults will pin the blame on the freak or weird kid involved in these sorts of events, which is why it is so important that you make it clear by your behavior that you are the blameless party in the incident.)

Of course, if the harassment becomes violent, then you've got an even bigger problem. Again, try to walk (or run, if necessary) to a different location, preferably where there are crowds of people and hopefully a few sane adults. If this isn't possible (and the Lady of the Manners is aware that sometimes it isn't), then you have to make the uncomfortable and *very quick* decision about whether you are capable of defending yourself. The Lady of the Manners doesn't like advocating violence, but if your tormentors seem intent on hurting you, do what you must to protect yourself. But she very strongly recommends reading up on the laws of your city (and school rules) concerning assault and battery, and to remember that while sharp pointy jewelry and metal lunch box handbags are fun accessories, if used in a fight they can possibly land you an assault with a deadly weapon charge, even if you didn't start the fight.

Lots of schools now have policies in place to help stop "bullying." The Lady of the Manners has no idea how effective any of those policies are but thinks they're a step in the right direction. If you are being harassed or tormented by classmates, don't be afraid to tell an adult and see if there are official steps you can take to make the harassment stop.

Keep in mind that your school years aren't forever; at times it may feel like they are, but eventually the time comes to an end. Just grit your teeth and concentrate on surviving so you can leave your herd-like classmates with their pack mentality far behind you.

Dealing with roommates

Roommates are quirky creatures. On the one hand, they can be your closest friends and confidants; on the other hand, they can be the evil things that borrow your clothes without asking first and leave the bathroom resembling a disaster area. Sometimes, they're all those things. The trick is to have roommates with more good qualities than bad and make sure that you don't unthinkingly annoy them as much as or more as they annoy you.

Now, while the above is true for roommates from all walks of life, a Goth on a quest for a roommate may have some unique concerns that your average folk don't run into. Take the topic of home decorating as a starting example. Yes, regular folks have to negotiate with their roommates about how the shared living quarters will look, just like Goths do. However, non-Goths probably don't have to have a conversation that covers points like, "Do you mind if I hang mounted and framed dead animals on the walls?" or "Oh, while you were out I decided to paint the walls glossy black" or "I've replaced all the regular lightbulbs with red ones." When you get a new roommate, make sure she doesn't have any decorating surprises in store and explain that you might have visitors who wouldn't appreciate the morbid charm of animal skulls hung on the walls. Also, if you live in a rented domicile, make sure everyone is aware of what the landlord considers damage and what the penalties may be. Though painting the walls red and purple may be a great idea, think hard about whether you're willing to give up your share of the damage deposit.

Almost all housemates have to set boundaries for borrowing each other's clothes. However, in an all-Goth household, it isn't so

Don't worry, Snarklings, the Lady of the Manners wouldn't allude to these housekeeping tips without sharing her information with you.

Removing candle wax: *You will need an iron and some brown paper grocery bags. Set the iron on a low heat/no steam setting and cut apart the grocery bags so they are flat pieces. Place one of the pieces on top of the wax-stained fabric and gently sweep the iron over the bag. The heat of the iron will slowly melt the wax and the paper bag will absorb it. Unless you are dealing with a very small amount of wax, you may need to move the paper bag around or use more than one piece. As with all household cleaning tasks, first test this procedure on a small, preferably unnoticeable section of the fabric just to make sure that it won't scorch or melt.*

Removing wine stains: *First, blot up the spill as soon as possible—cloth towels work much better than paper towels for this. Don't rub—that will merely make the stain larger. After blotting, cover the stain with a layer of salt, add a small amount of warm water to the stain, and let it sit; the salt should absorb most of the stain. If the stain has already set, mix some dishwashing detergent (the Lady of the Manners has been assured that either liquid or powdered detergent will work) with hydrogen peroxide and gently wash and rinse the affected area. (Again, test the cleaning mixture on an unnoticeable section for colorfastness, blah, blah, blah, you should know the drill.)*

Removing hair dye from bathroom surfaces: *Baby wipes. Yes, the Lady of the Manners is serious. She (and count-*

less other Goths) have discovered that baby wipes are very good at removing dye stains from one's skin and the countertops. If the baby wipes don't remove the spots of color from assorted bathroom surfaces, that's when it's time to break out something like OxiClean or one of the Magic Eraser cleaning "sponges." Do not, for goodness' sake, use the Magic Eraser to remove stains from yourself! (Oh, you may laugh, Snarklings, but the Lady of the Manners has heard some sad tales about such so-called "clever" notions.) If the baby wipes don't seem to be removing the stains left on your skin, try makeup remover. Also, hair dye likes to stick to soap scum. It may seem counterintuitive to scrub out the tub or shower before you apply hair color, but trust the Lady of the Manners when she says that it does save cleaning time in the long run. Like wine, hair dye spatters and spills should be cleaned up as soon as possible.

Removing the lingering odors of cigarettes or incense: Fill a spray bottle with cheap vodka (the Lady of the Manners means really cheap vodka) mixed with water and spray it around the room, on the furniture, or on items of clothing. (If you're misting down clothing, let the garment air out before putting it back in the closet.) The mixture should be one-half to two-thirds vodka, and the rest water. This trick can also be used to clean and deodorize fragile or hard-to-clean garments. (For the younger Snarklings who are not yet legally allowed to buy cheap, awful vodka, commercially available products such as Febreze do essentially the same thing. They just come with additional "fresh scent" fragrances.)

much about raiding closets as it is about figuring out whose black lace skirt is whose. It's all well and good to have a roommate whose taste in clothing complements yours, but it makes sorting laundry a bit difficult. Sewing nametags into your clothing is one tedious option, though most people just make each roommate responsible for his or her own laundry, thus avoiding the whole "Are these your stripy tights or mine?" quandary.

Goth housekeeping also presents its own unique set of problems. Goths who are planning on sharing a house or apartment with others should be armed with the knowledge of how to remove candle wax from shag carpeting, wine stains from upholstery, the lingering smell of cigarettes and incense from a room, and hair dye stains from any bathroom surface. (Upon reflection, even Goths who live on their own should probably know all those things, just to make their home a tidier place.) Other general rules roommates should discuss when first setting up house together:

- **A house policy on overnight guests.** The thrill of meeting naked strangers in your own bathroom wears out after a while. Try to make sure that you don't spring surprise guests on your housemates. Contrariwise, make sure not to barge in on a roommate when he or she is . . . er . . . occupied with company. Always knock first, even when you're sure your roommate's just reading or playing *World of Warcraft*.

- **A house policy on long-term romantic entanglements.** One group of the Lady of the Manners's friends has the rule that boyfriends and girlfriends who regularly spend more than three nights a week at the house have to contribute to the rent. Some people don't want their roommate's romantic partner to spend the night at all, while other people just want a rough idea of how often to expect it. Try to set up guidelines, even if none of the people sharing living quarters are involved with anyone at the time. Situations change, and it's easier to have an idea of how things should work before everyone gets all dewy-eyed with new romance and lust.

- **An emergency rule for music.** While no one person should dictate the soundtrack of a living arrangement, it is helpful to know that if you are in the throes of sleeplessness or a high-stress work week, you can respectfully request that your room-mate not play certain music that might aggravate things. The same rule must apply to all roommates, with the person experiencing the greater level of stress or chaos getting the ultimate vote. However, that does not mean that a roommate should get away with playing the latest Count von SpookyBat CD at top volume at three a.m. because she's "upset." Being upset does not mean, under any circumstances, that you get to deprive others of their much-needed rest.

A general idea of what sorts of behavior are acceptable. Some people wouldn't mind at all if their room-mate decided to start running a fetish photography business out of the house; others might strenuously object. If you aren't sure about what a roommate's reaction might be, ask. Don't leave little notes on the refrigerator after the fact, don't casually mention, "Oh, I'm throwing a big party," on the day of the event, and don't spontaneously rearrange the furniture while the roommates are out of town. Just don't.

A set date when the household bills are to be paid. Yes, even if you just have to have a new outfit or concert tickets, the bills must be paid, and preferably on time. Room-mates who routinely neglect this important idea should be asked to find a new place to live sooner rather than later.

A plan for how household chores will be split up. It is very disheartening to come home to a dirty kitchen because you've only just discovered that your roommate loves to cook but can't stand to do dishes. Deciding in advance who will do which tasks is far better than standing in a dirty bathroom screaming at each other, and a checklist of house-hold tasks can ensure that the cat box does get cleaned in a timely manner.

Other things potential Goth roommates should ask each other? Oh, the usual run-down: likes, dislikes, sexual orientation (just so there are no surprises), vegetarian or not, and so on. Do be sure to talk about pets with about-to-be-housemates; it's only fair to people who have allergies or, in the case of more unusual pets, phobias. In other words, don't assume that everyone will be as fond of your pet tarantula or snake as you are.

FIVE

Gothy Clichés and Why They're So Pervasive

Cliché. If you spend any time at all in the Goth subculture, you will hear that term thrown about, and it is almost never meant in a kind way. Having someone call you a cliché can be a bit mortifying, partially because "cliché" has a pervasive undercurrent of bad pantomime about it. Whoever throws the term around probably feels that you are more than faintly ridiculous. That you've gone right past the black velvet horizon and are slinking toward bad parody.

Let's look at the definition for cliché, shall we?

Cliché

 A trite, stereotyped expression; a sentence or phrase usually expressing a popular or common thought or idea that has lost originality, ingenuity, and impact by long overuse, as *sadder but wiser*, or *strong as an ox*.

🦇 (In art, literature, drama, etc.) a trite or hackneyed plot, character development, use of color, musical expression, etc.

🦇 Anything that has become trite or commonplace through overuse.

Ah-ha! Trite, commonplace, overused, and unoriginal! Well, no wonder people (and especially Goths) get so upset about being called a cliché!

However, clichés are the dirty little secrets at the heart of Gothdom. No, the Lady of the Manners is serious about this. Most Goth styles are based on specific archetypes, and that fact is a thorn in the side of many people in the subculture. Everyone wants to believe he or she is a beautiful and unique creature, not some silly person who wears black and reads a lot of books about vampires. But hardly anyone sprang forth, fully formed, from the brow of Peter Murphy or Siouxsie Sioux, with perfectly applied eyeliner and an artistically melancholy and dramatic nature. Even the Lady of the Manners, who as a child wanted to grow up to marry Dracula or become the Wicked Witch of the West, paid her dues as a semi-clueless and overly earnest babybat.

Clichés are what make the ElderGoths roll their eyes at the babybats, even though the younger generation is just doing the same silly stuff the ElderGoths did years ago. And yes, the Lady of the Manners can already hear some of you asking, "But if it's the same sort of stuff, why is it now okay to make fun of it?"

The answer is, it isn't really okay to make fun of it, but people do. (Yes, even the Lady of the Manners has rolled her eyes and made quietly snarky comments to friends about other people's eyeliner or poorly applied whiteface.) You see, many people become uncomfortable when presented with living, breathing examples of how they behaved in the throes of youthful fervor. ElderGoths (usually) like to present themselves as terribly jaded and (again, usually) ennui-laden. "Oh, how *adorable*," they'll say in sarcasm-laden tones, "*Look at that one with all the swirly eyeliner. Isn't that . . . cute.*" Nothing will make an ElderGoth turn snippy and sarcastic faster than seeing someone indulging in stereotypical Goth behavior or "costumes," because the more senior members want to believe that they (and the Goth culture) have moved beyond the instantly recognizable and lampoonable trademarks of Goth. With, sometimes, a smidgen of resentment that they themselves don't feel they can indulge in those overused icons for fear of looking like someone who is new to Goth. What are some of those instantly recognizable trademarks, those overused icons, those . . . clichés? Read on Snarklings, read on . . .

Why Friends don't let friends dress like the Crow

Ah, *The Crow*. Long ago, a new comic book appeared. Rendered in black and white, it was a violent, anguished story of lost love, and it was not your typical comic book story. It bracketed nightmarish images of despair and bloody retribution with poetry by Rimbaud and lyrics by The Cure and Joy Division. Word of mouth caused interest in the comic to grow amongst the black-clad types, until it began to seem that all Goths were required to have a copy (along with your tattered paperback of *Interview with the Vampire*, Sandman comics, dried roses, black boots, white face powder, and assorted eyeliner pencils). But even with the

comic's near ubiquitousness amongst Goths, it still seemed like an "insider" sort of thing. If you saw someone reading an issue, you could (kind of) safely assume that the reader shared at least some of your interests and would understand the things you held close to your black romantic heart. This sort of thinking carried over, to a degree, when you saw someone in Crow makeup at a club or convention. Dressing like the Crow almost became a sub-cultural shorthand indicating a person's interests in other comics, movies, books, and music.

As time went by, the comic gained a higher profile in pop culture and then, lo and behold, the movie was made. And as adaptations go, the movie was pretty good. Brandon Lee did a stunning job, and his death was a tragic loss. But the movie brought the story of *The Crow* even higher visibility; the subsequent sequels, spin-off comics and novels, and TV show got even more attention. It wasn't a cult-following thing anymore—it suddenly seemed like just about everyone knew about *The Crow*. Which meant that people who weren't hard-core fans began co-opting the look. That was fine and dandy, for fashion is always about borrowing an idea you like and making it your own. But people weren't just taking inspiration from the imagery and adding it to their look; they were slapping on some whiteface and black lipstick and drawing black triangles around their eyes. Things got to the point where you couldn't go to a Goth club without seeing a flock of Crow-wannabes, most of whom had applied their makeup in a ham-fisted manner. The Crow is one of those classic "insta-Goth" icons, but he has an easier look to copy than Dracula. Almost everyone recognizes it (those who don't probably assume the costumed person is impersonating someone from pro-wrestling or a black metal band), which is why people who want to play tourist and visit one of those "weird clubs with all the freaky people in black" pull on some black jeans, a black T-shirt, and a trench coat, slap on some black and white makeup, and head out, feeling confident that they'll "blend in." They don't. The idea is also being appropriated by people who aren't quite Goth, but SpoOoOKy. That is part of where the clichéd aspect of dressing like the Crow comes from, but there's another layer to the clichés.

Dressing like the Crow is also one of the great starter-Goth traditions; it's pretty much the male equivalent of dressing like Death from the Sandman comics, which almost every fledgling Goth girl does at least once. Again, it's that shortcut to spooooookiness that is the attraction. A pre-formed identity

If you ever go to a Marilyn Manson concert (or some other I am dark and dangerous and EVIL! type of band), you can have a lot of fun by playing "Spot the Crow." The last time the Lady of the Manners played this game, she counted sixteen Crows in one stadium.

that allows the costumed person to feel not only Dark and Mysterious but as if he is part of an alternative subculture (while all he's really done is broadcast that he isn't as connected to that alternative subculture as he thinks).

Eventually people who settle into the Goth world and feel at home there stop needing those pre-formed identities and masks. They feel comfortable being themselves and not adopting what they thought was a required template. (And then they probably go on to mock other people who are new to the scene and experimenting with appropriating the same subcultural icons. It's a vicious circle, Snarklings.)

Over the years, the Lady of the Manners has gone on and on (and on and on and on and . . .) about how friends don't let friends dress like the Crow. Dressing up like the Crow is considered by most Goths to be trite, overdone, and a bit like holding up a sign that says, "mostly clueless." But you know what? The Lady of the Manners also thinks that if you really, really, *really* want to dress up like the Crow, you should do it. If that is what makes you happy, if you think that would be the coolest Halloween costume ever for you, then do it. The Lady of the Manners does, however, have two pieces of advice. First: Accept the fact that people will roll their eyes, snicker, laugh, and generally try to make you feel like an idiot. Ignore them. Second: Do the best job you can with the makeup and assembling the costume. Apply the whiteface makeup evenly (over every bit of exposed skin, please, and that includes your ears and neck), and make sure the eyeliner and black streaks are symmetrical. Think long and hard about whether you have the proper physique to wear the costume; it is a sad, harsh fact that nothing becomes an object of ridicule faster than a heavier-set person dressed up as a character previously portrayed by Brandon Lee.

There is nothing wrong with dressing like one of your idols. (The

Lady of the Manners dresses a bit like Mary Poppins's evil twin, which garners her some confused looks, so she wouldn't dream of telling someone not to dress like a fictional character.) So sure, go paint your face and put on your trench coat. Wind strips of electrical tape up your arms, even. Just understand that some people will assume you are trying to blend in with a subculture you aren't very informed about. Be prepared for snide looks and eye-rolling from some people, but do not let those snide looks diminish your enjoyment. Instead, smile back in a knowing (and, if you can manage it, faintly condescending) manner and then ignore them.

No, we don't all think we're vampires (but we do read a lot of vampire books)

"Listen to them, the children of the night. What music they make!"

That quote from *Dracula* has probably been applied to the modern Goth scene since it first crawled out of its fog-enshrouded lair, with strains of "Bela Lugosi's Dead" still ringing through the night sky. Yes, Snarklings, vampires and Goth have a long, long his-

tory together. How could they not? The Lady of the Manners can't think of a more quintessentially Goth archetype than a creature that is immortal, mesmerizing, and preternaturally alluring and seductive. The entire notion beckons languidly to just about anyone who leans toward the darkly decadent. Not to mention that the classic image of a vampire is an aristocrat wearing sumptuous clothing. All right, an aristocrat wearing sumptuous and possibly blood-splattered clothing, but still—he's wearing it in a darkly elegant sort of way.

You don't have to look very closely to see marks of the vampire scattered all throughout Goth culture. Coffin-shaped accessories, a fondness for bat motifs, clothing and makeup specifically designed to make us all look like we've risen from a well-appointed grave—is it any wonder that, to an outside eye, we just might look like we think we are those creatures of the night? Or at least desperately hope to become them?

Wanting to be a vampire is, of course, one of the classic fantasies. The power to compel people to do your bidding and use unnatural strength to vanquish your enemies with no pesky thoughts of mortality to trouble you is beguiling. There's also the flip side, the allure of being chosen the victim of a vampire. Not the sort of victim who is drained and abandoned in an unmarked grave, but someone with whom the vampire feels a strong connection. Someone who is so special that the vampire cannot bring himself to kill you but is still driven to feed from you and leave you swooning.

(Yes, Snarklings, most vampire fantasies *do* have a strong erotic thread. Why do you think there's been such a boom in the "preternatural romance" genre of late?)

The idea of being the special and cherished vampire victim ties directly into the idea that a vampire is the ultimate "bad boy" or "bad girl," someone with an exciting air of danger who everyone else misunderstands and avoids, but who is different with you. You have a connection with the vampire because you're different from the others and see through his tough façade. Only you can understand him! The Lady of the Manners has been involved in discussions with

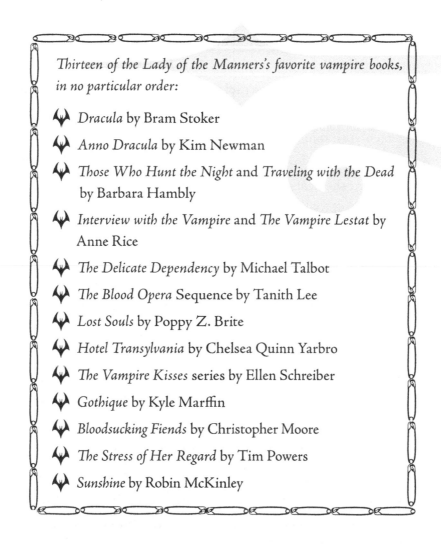

> *Thirteen of the Lady of the Manners's favorite vampire books, in no particular order:*
>
> *Dracula* by Bram Stoker
>
> *Anno Dracula* by Kim Newman
>
> *Those Who Hunt the Night* and *Traveling with the Dead* by Barbara Hambly
>
> *Interview with the Vampire* and *The Vampire Lestat* by Anne Rice
>
> *The Delicate Dependency* by Michael Talbot
>
> *The Blood Opera* Sequence by Tanith Lee
>
> *Lost Souls* by Poppy Z. Brite
>
> *Hotel Transylvania* by Chelsea Quinn Yarbro
>
> *The Vampire Kisses* series by Ellen Schreiber
>
> *Gothique* by Kyle Marffin
>
> *Bloodsucking Fiends* by Christopher Moore
>
> *The Stress of Her Regard* by Tim Powers
>
> *Sunshine* by Robin McKinley

other fans of vampire fiction about the quintessential "bad boy" appeal of the vampire, and the thing that all of us agree on is this: the personality traits that make a fictional vampire so interesting would not be so exciting to deal with in real life. In the real world, brooding types only you can understand, who hide their gentler, tender emotions from everyone but you (you special and magical creature, you), eventually will start treating you the same way they treat everyone else. Which means somewhat poorly, to say the least.

Oh, don't get the Lady of the Manners wrong, Snarklings. If pressed, the Lady of the Manners would have to admit that her favorite genre of fiction is vampire stories. Not only did the Lady of the Manners spend her late adolescence sighing over the vampire gang from *The Lost Boys*, but she still has a weakness for fictional gentlemen with fangs, an air of danger, and a menacing smile that possibly conceals a lonely heart. But she also gets just a bit concerned when she hears other people exclaiming rapturously over a fictional fanged bad boy, "Oh, he's the perfect man! I wish I could meet someone just like him."

Yet, if you were to ask a lot of Goths about their interest in vampires, many of them would scoff derisively and try to downplay the vampire influence in the Goth subculture. "Sure," a Goth may say, "'Bela Lugosi's Dead' was the catalyst for modern Goth culture, but we've moved beyond that. The only people who are into the whole vampire thing anymore are fang-bangers or gaming geeks." However, the Lady of the Manners is willing to bet at least a couple velvet cloaks and a coffin purse that a person who would say that doth protest just the teensiest bit too much.

Oh, an aside about the "fang-bangers or gaming geeks" comment: Yes, many Goths became a touch disenchanted with the whole notion of vampires when *Vampire: The Masquerade*, a roleplaying game by White Wolf, became popular. Suddenly it wasn't just Goths wearing fang prosthetics and dressing up; there were people whose only connection to Goth came from a gaming book, who were coming into the clubs and playing characters. To many

Goths, that seemed silly and disrespectful. The Lady of the Manners, who freely admits to having participated in vampire RPGs, thinks that the Goths who are cranky about the LARPers (er, Live-Action Role Players) need to calm down. Yes, it is a little annoying to have someone treat you as a character in a game in which you're not involved, but there's no need to be pissy about it. The people playing vampire games aren't, on the whole, mocking the Goth subculture. They're just interested in a good story.

However, the Lady of the Manners has a gentle reminder for those readers who participate in vampire role-playing games: don't involve people who aren't part of the game. The Lady of the Manners understands the temptation, but trying to force non-players' participation in your imaginary world is not polite and may possibly get you booted out of the Goth club. Every LARP the Lady of the Manners has ever heard of always wore something that signified participation in the game; always remember to look for that token, and don't annoy the people who are looking for nothing more dramatic than an evening out.

Another reason many Goths are so derisive about the allure of the vampire is that there is indeed a flourishing vampire subculture, and while it shares many stylistic markers with Goth, the two aren't the same. The vampire (or vampyre, as the Lady of the Manners has seen it spelled to identify the subculture) community is strongly interested in all aspects and manifestations of vampires and vampirism, be it energy vampirism (psychic vampires) or blood-drinkers (sanguine vampires). Some members of the vampire community participate in blood play and blood drinking. Wait! Stop looking so alarmed! People who are part of the vampyre subculture *do not* go out and attack people. Blood play activities are done between consenting adults. The sanguine vampire types aren't out to find victims. "Consenting adults" is the important phrase there, by the way. The Lady of the Manners did a bit of research and wasn't able to find *anything* implying that those blood play activities are illegal, as long as the participants agreed to them. Of course, laws vary from state to state and country to country, so if you want to explore sanguinary vampires and blood play, the Lady of the Manners strongly encourages you to do your own research.

Even with Goths wanting to differentiate themselves from vampyres and vampire LARPers, the vampire archetype still holds a strong allure for those of us in the black-clad and spooky world. Almost every Goth will be fond of at least one or two vampire novels or movies, and the opening drums of "Bela Lugosi's Dead" will drag even a hesitant ElderGoth onto the dance floor time and time again. But that doesn't mean we think we're really vampires, or even that vampires are real. But they do have nice clothes . . .

No, you don't have to be depressed to be a Goth

"You can't be a Real Goth; you're too happy." If the Lady of the Manners had a nickel for every time someone has said that to her, she would probably be able to go off and buy some brand new Fluevog boots. If you mention "Goth" to someone outside the subculture, the image that springs to mind almost always includes a black-clad, morose creature writing sad poetry by candlelight. Those who don't understand our community believe that Goths are never happy, that we are gloomy and delicate little flowers that feel the pain of the world. But why?

Remember, modern Goth culture has its inky-black roots in

melodrama. Yes, Goth not only tends toward the dark, the morbid, and the unearthly but positively wallows in it. The morbid outlook, the fondness for looking as if we're off to attend a funeral (or were recently the guest of honor at one); those things, to an outsider's eyes, give the impression that not only are Goths fond of gloom and doom but that we devote ourselves to it entirely and are incapable or unwilling to entertain the faintest glimmer of a smile.

Which is ridiculous, of course. While Goths do appreciate a certain amount of picturesque melancholic languishing, they do not sign a contract promising to be despondent and tragic at all times. Goths, on the whole, actually are fairly cheerful and up-beat individuals. They just have a healthy dose of black humor and whimsy and a dark-hued wardrobe to match it.

The belief that all Goths are depressed is often coupled with the somewhat contradictory but just as prevalent idea that all

Goths are gleefully entranced with death. It goes something like, we all think death, despair, and destruction are amazingly cool and nifty, but we're too dismal to talk about it. Instead, we retreat to our black-painted rooms, cry a lot, and compose poetry about death and graveyards, possibly written in our own blood. None of this is really true, but it is such a powerful cliché that people believe it. Goths are, on the whole, somewhat fascinated by death and morbid imagery because Goths realize that just because something is morbid or unsettling doesn't mean it should be dismissed or ignored. By refusing to turn a blind eye to the brevity of one's mortal existence, Goths are able to search out beauty in dark or unusual places. In the Lady of the Manners's eyes, that doesn't make one depressed and obsessed with death; instead it allows one to fully embrace life.

So you say you're not a Goth, but people keep assuming you are

There are swarms and swarms of people out there who wear all black, are interested in graveyards, gargoyles, and horror fiction, or just prefer a darker aesthetic, but they still maintain they aren't Goths. Sometimes this is because they believe the rather sensationalist portrayal of Goths by the media and feel that Goths are much more disturbed, depressed, or just plain weird. "Oh, no, I'm not a Goth. Goths are way freakier than I am. I just like [fill in the blank with a gothy-type interest here]." Or they may feel that Goth is something only teenagers do because it's "just a phase." Or that they aren't Goths because they don't dress in a dark extravagant manner or listen to all Goth music all the time.

All of these explanations do make sense, but they still amuse the Lady of the Manners. These explanations make it sound like one must match a minimum number of Goth habits and traits on some master list before calling oneself a Goth. Or that a multiple-choice test can determine someone's subcultural preferences and Goths take it with the goal of racking up as many Goth points as possible.

Of course, some people complain about being labeled Goth; they don't want to be labeled at all. Labels are restrictive and so limiting! Sure, these people may share dark and mysterious interests with the rest of us black-clad spooksters, but they refuse to be labeled. They can get terribly resentful because they believe there's so much more to their personalities and lives than can be encompassed by a (gasp, shudder of revulsion) label.

The Lady of the Manners hates to be the bearer of harsh news to these charming people, but they need to get over it. Labels can be used in a derogatory fashion, but that's not what the Lady of the Manners is talking about here. The Lady of the Manners wants to talk about the relatively harmless use of labels as a form of social shorthand. (The Lady of the Manners has noticed that the people who make the biggest fuss about being labeled are usually quick to label other people. "Norms." "Yuppies." "Bimbos." "Jocks." Labels are only distasteful when applied to their oh-so-complex selves. Think about that for a bit, Snarklings.)

Labels are useful because they express a whole bundle of information in a compact little package. Labels can be explained and expanded upon, if need be, to communicate all nuances and quirks of personality, but sometimes brevity is a splendid thing. Labels can help sketch the broad outlines of a person and his or her interests. The Lady of the Manners doesn't mind being called a Goth, a clothes fiend, or even eccentric because she knows that all of those labels do, in one way or another, describe facets of her personality. They're not the *only* facets of the Lady of the Manners's personality, but they are some of the more obvious ones, and fussing about that would be just plain silly.

People are, for the most part, social creatures who like to sort themselves into "us" and "them" groupings. This is not out of any sense of exclusion, really, but because people tend to feel more comfortable around others who share their interests. People identify themselves by their favorite sports teams, by their political party, by what musical groups or TV shows they like, or perhaps by the hobbies they enjoy (knitting, hiking, poker . . . you get the idea).

If you wear all black, listen to obscure bands, and have a generally dark and decadent aesthetic, then of course people are going to label you a Goth. Does that mean you are a Goth? Maybe, maybe not, but it's probably a good bet that you share certain interests with Goths. Getting all wound up about being labeled is a waste of time and energy that could instead be used toward developing other aspects of your lifestyle or personality so people stop calling you a Goth, if that's what you want. And even if people don't stop calling you a Goth, is that really so bad? The Lady of the Manners is sure there are far worse things someone could call you.

The roots of Goth's dark garden

Oh, so you want to learn more about Goth clichés and where they come from? The Lady of the Manners in no way claims this section provides an exhaustive list of gothy reference materials, but it can be a jumping-off point for your own research. Don't worry, Snarklings. While the Lady of the Manners *could* just tell you to seek out "Gothic literature" at your local library, she wants to encourage you in your search with the information below. But speaking of Gothic literature, yes, you should read at least a few of the classic works.

🦇 *Jane Eyre* by Charlotte Brontë. This is perhaps *the* Gothic novel; it's jam-packed with plucky orphans, uncaring and unkind relatives, grim boarding schools and wicked teachers, and characters who die tragically of consumption. Jane herself becomes a governess in a house that suffers from mysterious laughter, outbreaks of fire, piercing and unexplained screams in the night, and a brooding, distant gentleman with a secret. And that's not the entire story! The Lady of the Manners won't spoil some of the more outlandish plot twists for you but will admit that she tends to view *Jane Eyre* as a black-tinged camp romp. Oh, the Lady of the Manners knows that's not how the novel is commonly regarded, but the Lady of the Manners reads *Jane Eyre* much later in life, not during her impressionable teens.

🦇 *Dracula* by Bram Stoker. The king of the vampires's shadow still looms over us, so do yourself a favor and read the book that has contributed so much to the Goth subculture. Yes, portions of it are meandering and tedious, but just as many sections still cast a strong spell over the reader.

🦇 *Frankenstein* by Mary Shelley. Considered by many to be the first true science fiction novel, this book also gave life to the mad scientist genre. (You do know that the creature isn't the one named Frankenstein, yes? The title refers to Doctor Victor Frankenstein, and his creation should be called Frankenstein's creature. Ignore popular culture's frequent mistake, and go read the book yourself.)

🦇 Anything by Edgar Allan Poe. The Lady of the Manners prefers *The Fall of the House of Usher* and "The Raven," but really, just about anything by Poe will fill out your shadowy-tinged reading list.

What if you want to read books that are a little more modern?

🦇 The Sandman series of graphic novels by Neil Gaiman. The Sandman series has been described as "the comic book for intellectuals" and has won all sorts of awards. But, more important, the series is a fantastic, multi-layered, and com-

Gothic Charm School

pelling story that blends classic and contemporary my-
thology, humor, fantasy, and horror. Morpheus, the King
of Dreams, is the anthropomorphic personification of
dreams. His "siblings" are Destiny, Death, Desire, Despair,
Delirium, and one other whose identity is a mystery for
a large part of the series. Death, with her tousled black
hair, punky black clothes, elaborate black eyeliner, and silver ankh pendant, has become as much of an archetype of
Goth girl appearance as Siouxsie Sioux.

- Anything by H.P. Lovecraft. Regarded by many as the father
  of modern horror fiction, the tentacles of his shadowy versions of cosmic horror and dread nameless gods are still
  coiled around parts of the Goth subculture.

- Any of the illustrated works of Edward Gorey. Why yes,
  the man who brought us *The Gashlycrumb Tinies* (a series of
  charmingly morbid rhymes about children who come to un-
  timely ends) is a huge influence on the modern Goth, and
  rightly so.

- *Something Wicked This Way Comes* by Ray Bradbury. Innocence, innocence lost, and *the* quintessential spooky travel-
  ing carnival are all important parts of this book. The Lady
  of the Manners rereads *Something Wicked This Way Comes*
  every October.

- *Lost Souls* by Poppy Z. Brite. Vampires, but not of the broodingly romantic type, and one of the first books to correctly
  capture and portray some aspects of Goth club culture.

If you feel like taking a break from reading, perhaps you'd like
to watch a few movies.

- *The Addams Family* and *Addams Family Values.* They're creepy,
  they're spooky, they're definitely ooky, and they're possibly
  one of the most charming and happy families you will ever see.
  Almost every Goth cherishes a flicker of hope that one day he
  or she will end up in a relationship as passionate and loving as
  Morticia and Gomez's. And yes, most Goths would like to live
  in a gloomy mansion and have a severed hand as a pet.

- *Dracula.* Both the Tod Browning and the Francis Ford Coppola versions, if you please. Neither of them is faithful to the novel (the Lady of the Manners dreams of someone deciding to make a big-budget mini-series out of the novel), but both contain iconic images that are repeated and re-interpreted throughout Gothdom.

- *Nosferatu*, the original 1922 version directed by F.W. Murnau. Loosely based on the novel of *Dracula*, *Nosferatu* gives us the long-lingering image of Max Schreck in all of his bat-eared, long-fingered spooky glory as Count Orlok. (Fun bonus fact: "schreck" is the German word for fright or terror.)

- *Metropolis*, directed by Fritz Lang. A science fiction tale filmed in 1927 and set in 2026, it features a story of class struggle and rebellion, mistaken identity, and robot doppelgangers, all set against a striking Art Deco backdrop.

- *The Nightmare Before Christmas.* The citizens of Halloweentown are responsible for the yearly spooky celebration of Halloween. But Jack Skellington, the Pumpkin King, is dissatisfied and wants something more. He goes wandering and discovers another place, where the inhabitants merrily work toward bringing forth Christmas every year. From that point, things go a bit awry, but with the best of intentions. Created in stop-motion animation, *The Nightmare Before Christmas* helped secure creator Tim Burton's role as a gothy visionary. Not to mention that the soundtrack, besides giving Goths their own version of Christmas carols to sing, was created by Danny Elfman, who before he turned to movie scores was in Oingo Boingo, a band much beloved by Goths.

- *Beetlejuice.* Lydia Deetz, the black-clad teen heroine of the movie, proclaims that her "life is a darkroom—one big . . . dark . . . room." Add in some ghosts trying to get Lydia's family out of the house and one chaotic "Bio-Exorcist," and you have a movie that has been a Goth classic for over two decades.

Speaking of music . . . if someone were to ask the Lady of the

Manners what Goth music they should explore, this is what she would recommend:

- *Staring at the Sea: The Singles 1979–1985* and *Disintegration* by The Cure

- *A Slight Case of Overbombing* by The Sisters of Mercy

- *Twice Upon a Time: The Singles* by Siouxsie and the Banshees

- *Crackle* by Bauhaus

- *Phantasmagoria* by The Damned

- *Serpentine Gallery* by Switchblade Symphony

- *Into the Labyrinth* by Dead Can Dance

- *Let Love In* by Nick Cave and the Bad Seeds

- *A Life Less Lived: The Gothic Box* from Rhino Records featuring various artists.

Why being called a cliché isn't such a bad thing

There is nothing wrong with being fond of things or having interests that others call clichéd. If they make you happy, what does it matter? The Lady of the Manners thinks everyone should strive to be his or her own person and not to be so wrapped up in What Other People Think. So other Goths roll their eyes because you want to picnic in the graveyard and live your life as if you were a member of the Addams Family—so what? The Lady of the Manners has finally reached the point where she tries very hard not to be as snarky about people embodying various gothy clichés because she herself is a walking collection of them: looking like she escaped from a Tim Burton movie, holding a strong belief that adding bats and black lace trim are always good design decisions, etc. Not only does the Lady of the Manners now derive quite a bit of amusement from her over-the-top moments of gothness, but she tries to hone and refine the more clichéd aspects of herself in order to make them the more perfect examples of those clichés. It's quite fun, actually.

The Lady of the Manners really does believe that if most of the Snarklings out there in GothyLand would just accept that the whole of Goth is kind of silly and amusing, there would be a lot less angst. That doesn't mean you shouldn't throw yourself into your black-clad, candlelit life wholeheartedly. No, not at all! What it does mean is that you should not only accept that people might poke fun at you but also should be willing to do so yourself. By accepting aspects of yourself that might be considered clichés, you take the power away from people throwing that word around with the intent to upset you. If someone calls you a cliché, raise an eyebrow at her and smile gently. After all, the line between cliché and archetype is very narrow; even if you don't want to transform your interests into quintessential gothy icons and archetypes, those interests are still interesting. Wrap yourself in black velvet, read ghost stories by candlelight while sipping absinthe, and feel smug about the fact that the people who would call you a cliché are probably too wrapped up in worrying about what other people might think about them to enjoy themselves as much as you are at that moment.

SIX

Goths and Romance

In case it somehow escaped your notice, romance is a rather essential part of the Goth mindset. No, the Lady of the Manners doesn't mean romance as exemplified by a certain genre of books with covers that feature the color pink, flowers, or "sassy" cartoons that tend to focus on shoes. Nor is she talking about another subgenre of books featuring young ladies in flowing nightdresses running away from broodingly handsome men, possibly on horseback, with some sort of picturesque ruin of a manor house or castle in the background. (Though those sorts of books are slightly closer to the Goth concept of romance.) No, what the Lady of the Man-

ners is talking about is a sense of mystery and excitement, the sort of intensity romance can bring. The way it invokes a sense of lushness, of flights of fancy, and strong emotions. In other words, when Goths talk about romance, they quite probably are thinking of these sorts of definitions:

- A quality or feeling of mystery, excitement, and remoteness from everyday life.

- A novel or other prose narrative depicting heroic or marvelous deeds, pageantry, romantic exploits, etc., usually in a historical or imaginary setting.

- The colorful world, life, or conditions depicted in such tales.

Does that mean Goths scoff at the more mainstream, hearts 'n' flowers version of romance? Of course not. Goths *revel* in that sort of thing, if in a slightly darker way than other people. Exchanging longing and/or smoldering looks across a candlelit table? Blood-red roses, walks in the moonlight, pining away in your darkened room over the person you adore—who may or may not know you exist—while listening to wildly emotional music? Oh, please, those are some of the very foundations of the Gothic mindset.

Etiquette for and about crushes

While Goths have a reputation for being gloomy and depressed all the time, that doesn't mean members of the black-clad underground are immune to crushes and twitterpation. (Twitterpation: attraction; causes fluttering in the tummy, silly grins to spread across the face, and almost full-time cases of distraction. You know how in cartoons a character's eyes go all heart-shaped, or little birds fly around his head when he's taken leave of his senses? That, Snarklings, is twitterpation.) And just like the rest of humanity, many Goths have no clue how to express their feelings or determine whether the object of their affections feels the same way. Now, the Lady of the Manners doesn't claim to be able to provide a checklist that would make everything clear, such as:

- Given or received flowers—Y/N

- Was asked out to a picnic in a graveyard—Y/N

- Lingering hugs good-bye—Y/N

But she does have some suggestions about dealing with crushes—having one, being the object of one, and how to behave gracefully in either situation.

You may have noticed feelings of fluttery uncertainty whenever you're around a particular someone. She makes you feel all silly and bouncy whenever she's near, but you haven't worked up the nerve to do more than burble endlessly about her to your friends. What to do, what to do? If you're already acquainted with this person, try to increase your social interaction; group outings to clubs, movies, and concerts are a good place to start. Also, if you're both part of the same social circle, you can try to make the Goth scene's ever-present gossip network work for you: have your friends subtly try to find out what her friends are saying about you. While you shouldn't take gossip as gospel, it is a good way of getting at least a vague idea of what your crush is thinking (or at least what your crush's friends are thinking). However, try not to resort to the completely transparent and juvenile tactic of having a friend tell the object of your affection of your interest. (No, even if you're a younger

Goth suffering through your first pangs of attraction, you shouldn't stoop to this tactic.) Nor should you post pages and pages of cryptic entries about your crush on your blog or Live-Journal. Remember that ever-present gossip network the Lady of the Manners mentioned just a few sentences ago? That gossip network *thrives* on such cryptic blog posts and will quite happily make up and assign all sorts of meanings to your posts. Not only that, but that ever-present gossip network will then spread new and exciting (and possibly unflattering) rumors about you.

Which leads us to a question: "Should I tell him that I, you know, like him? *Like* him like him?" Well, probably. Keep in mind that your behavior has probably telegraphed your interest in this person to most of your friends already, no matter how circumspect you think you've been. It is one of the cornerstones of the universe: if you have a crush on someone, you are incapable of acting normal around him or her. Don't look at the Lady of the Manners like that and insist you have treated your crush the same way you treat all your friends. You may think you have, but just trust the Lady of the Manners on this one, okay? She's not saying you've started behaving like the clueless-but-endearing lead character in a stereotypical romantic comedy, but there is no way

> *The Lady of the Manners is well aware that gossip networks and drama storms exist in every social community. But the Goth scene seems to be particularly drama-prone. Is it because all of us black-clad romantics want life to be so much more interesting than it seems? The Lady of the Manners suspects the drama comes from that, along with the close-knit nature of the Goth scene and the strongly held opinions spooky types want to make people aware of, even if only by whispering them in ill-lit nightclubs.*

on earth that you've managed to appear completely cool and collected.

So where does that leave you? After a few weeks or so, the object of your affection might be showing subtle signs you can try to interpret (or ask your friends to interpret, if you're really unsure). Long daily e-mail exchanges, increased social activities, and lingering hugs can usually mean, "I am responding to your interest in me. Now ask me out or kiss me or something."

(The Lady of the Manners says "usually" here because she is well aware that some people out there like to collect crushes and flirtations. Nothing makes these people happier than a string of besotted admirers following them around. While that in and of itself is not a bad thing, it does make an admirer heartsore and weary after a while. If you suspect that this is happening to you, tactfully quiz mutual friends and find out if the object of your affection is the sort of person who likes to play "collect the set." If the answer is yes, then you will probably be better off if you ruthlessly quash your attraction and stay just friends, no matter how difficult it seems.)

Some signals can be difficult to interpret. Your crush might say things like, "I don't think I'm cut out for dating," "I'm happy being single," or "I don't want to date anyone for a long time" (which is something the Lady of the Manners said to her then-future husband when they first started socializing). This doesn't mean this person is crazy. It might just mean (a) your crush wants to be pursued slowly, (b) your crush doesn't know what he or she wants, which means you have a chance, or (c) your crush feels the need to say that for the sake of pride. Once you notice this sort of behavior, for heaven's sake, ask the object of your affection out. Ask him out to coffee or tea, ask if she'd like to go on a midnight picnic, ask if he'd like to go to the movies. But ask, and make it clear that you are asking about a romantic date-like activity. Don't waffle, don't write pages and pages of agonized ponderings about whether or not you should. While romantic comedies are rife with scenarios where two people are interested in each other but too shy to do anything about it until fate throws them together, those situations tend not to happen very often in the nonfiction world.

But what if you're the object of someone's affection? The suspicion has started to dawn on you that someone thinks of you in a special manner. Friends are starting to whisper and giggle, and apparently you have been given the superpower to cause a specific person to blush and become tongue-tied. Now what do you do?

The simple answer is to treat the smitten person in the same manner that *you* would like to be treated if the positions were reversed. Sending out subtle signals (such as the ones mentioned above) is one method. Others favor taking the direct route and just asking the smitten person out on a date. But what do you do when you really *do* just want to be friends with this person? You don't want to hurt his or her feelings. You want to be nice, but you don't see any possibility of a romantic entanglement.

This is where you have to keep a close watch over your own actions and comments. Try not to do or say anything that the person with the crush could misinterpret as encouragement. But what if you're good friends with this person? Try to become deliberately obtuse about his or her motives, and treat everything like a mere friendly gesture. Again, if possible, use the ever-present gossip network to subtly get the message out. (But make sure that the message doesn't come across as, "What are you, crazy?! Give it up—why would she be interested in you?!" You're just trying to dissuade your crush, not trample emotions and self-esteem.) The object, if at all possible, is to avoid having to deliver the "just friends" speech. No one likes being on the receiving end of that little talk, and it is almost always the kiss of death for a friendship.

The hope here is that the person with the crush gradually realizes the romantic feelings aren't being reciprocated and eventually finds someone else to pursue.

Unfortunately, sometimes the person with the crush doesn't catch on. No matter how clear you think you are being, your admirer keeps trying: visiting you at work, leaving you little presents, constantly inviting you out, worming into conversations you're having with other people, acting jealous—these are the actions of someone who isn't getting the hint. There is a line between expressing interest and stalking, and for some people that line blurs quite easily.

The best thing you can do is communicate that you don't feel comfortable with the level of attention. Try to explain this calmly, but don't be surprised if they doesn't quite get it. At that point, the only thing you can do is end your association. If you run into each other in a social situation, be distantly friendly: don't go over and get involved in a long conversation. Translation: just acknowledge their presence and then try not to interact with them.

Flirting and dating

Goths, preferring to think of themselves as creatures of dark romance, spend a lot of time wrapped up in flirting or dating. Those two things can be the source of fun, entertainment, and happiness, as well as a lot of angst, tortured internal monologues, and long phone calls or e-mails to close friends. However, that list of woes should not be prompted by glaring lapses in common courtesy by one or both parties. The Lady of the Manners has been shocked— shocked, she tells you—by some of the tales of tragedy that she has seen or heard of over the years.

Flirting is a traditional social activity in the Goth scene, especially at night clubs. However, what one person considers harmless flirting can be construed by another as "I find you very attractive and would like to get to 'know you better' in private." Sitting on people's laps, excessive touching, or kissing are generally considered to go beyond mere flirtation. If you indulge in this sort of behavior and then claim it "didn't mean anything," or, even worse, are confused about the level of companionship someone expects from you, don't be surprised if that someone gets upset. Of course, context is everything. Perhaps, for example, your social circle is much more casual about smooches and caresses. If that's the case, try to monitor your behavior when you're around people outside your usual circle. Don't feel you have to change your behavior, but be aware that others might interpret it differently. If that happens, don't feel embarrassed (or angry). Just try to explain.

What if you're from a social circle that doesn't casually smooch and fondle and are mixing with people who treat such behavior as commonplace? First, check with the person you know best at the gathering and ask what is going on. Don't feel you have to fumble blindly through things. Ask for context. Second, don't feel pressured to change your behavior to match everyone else's. If you don't want to spend the evening at the club making out with your friends, you don't have to. Don't get indignant or deliver a lecture; just make it clear (in a polite and friendly way, of course) that you have somewhat different boundaries and would like them respected.

When embarking upon a flirtation, be honest about your motives, if only to yourself. Have you recently ended another relationship and are merely looking for distraction and reassurance that others find you fascinating and attractive? There's nothing wrong with that, but, to avoid confusion, be very sure of the signals you're sending out. Also, flirting to make your current or ex romantic entanglement jealous is not nice. It's petty, it's unfair to innocent bystanders, and (repeatedly indulged) it's a sure way to prompt unkind gossip about yourself.

Those receiving the flirtation must remember that flirting does not automatically equal romantic potential. It's perfectly fine (and pleasant) to flirt back, but always ask before assuming that it means something more than just a friendly social diversion.

Do not interfere with others' flirting. If you think that one of the people flirting needs to be informed about the other's past behavior or preferences, stop and think seriously about whether you should be the one to deliver that information. Even if you decide you *are*, don't interrupt what is going on to do so, and be very tactful as to how you approach the topic.

If someone doesn't respond to your flirting, leave him or her alone. Some people may not always be in the mood to flirt, some aren't comfortable with flirtatious behavior at all, and some may not want to flirt with *you*. (Yes, the Lady of the Manners is certain that you're all charming and dashing, Snarklings, but sometimes people have odd tastes that can't be explained, or are entangled in situations that you may not know about.) If you want to ask out the object of your affection, then for heaven's sake just take the direct route and do it. Yes, that requires some courage on your part, but it's better than repeatedly making overtures to someone who hasn't noticed your oh-so subtle self, or (worse yet!) isn't really interested. It also saves a lot of angst and worrying over whether someone likes you or not.

Speaking of asking someone out, when the word "date" is applied to a social outing between two people, it means that at least one of you (and hopefully both of you) is thinking in terms of a possible romance. If you agree to go out on a date (especially after flirting with someone), do not be astonished if the other person considers the outing a stepping stone toward a relationship. If that was not your intention when you accepted the "date," make things clear by using a phrase like, "This was fun; you're a great *friend* to do things with." While no one likes getting the "I think of you as a friend" speech, it's still better than finding that what you thought was a budding romance was merely a friendly companionship.

If you have to miss a scheduled date, contact your companion *as soon as possible.* The only acceptable reason to stand someone up is a serious emergency, and you should explain what happened within twenty-four hours (unless you or someone very close to you is hospitalized). Suddenly having a change of heart, going out with someone else, or just forgetting . . . none of these are acceptable reasons. Even if you feel uncomfortable telling the person that you don't want to follow through with the date, you still should. If you didn't want to go out on the date, you shouldn't have accepted the invitation. If you didn't consider the invitation to be a "date," then you should have made that clear. Standing someone up for those (or similar) reasons is inexcusable.

Mind you, no one is *owed* a date, ever. The only reason you should accept a date (or whatever you want to call a romantic social activity between two people) is because you are interested in spending time together. You don't have to go out with someone just because he or she is nice, pays attention to you, or seems to expect it. Nor should you feel obligated to go out with someone because both of you are single Goths who know each other. You may scoff, Snarklings, but the Lady of the Manners has seen that exact thing happen with alarming regularity.

Do not accept dates merely to make former loves jealous or to distract yourself from current heartbreak. Yes, it is quite heady, while you are wallowing in the despair, to realize that someone (possibly new, possibly an old friend) finds you romantically enticing; letting that realization lead you into situations you may not yet be emotionally ready for, however, is asking for trouble.

Honestly, none of this is very difficult. In fact, it all boils down to that wonderful age-old standard: how would you feel if someone did this to you? The Lady of the Manners is frequently surprised by how many people (of all ages, though it is especially common amongst the younger set) don't think of their actions in that light because it's so simple. Of course, people have to be honest about their own behavior and think about how it might impact others, which is often tricky. Most people (whether they'll admit it or not) lean toward self-absorption, so thinking about how their actions will make others feel is a bit of a leap. There's also the sticky problem that no one likes to be the "bad guy" . . . if you don't think about someone else's reactions, then you won't have to suffer the stomach-churning feeling that you have done something wrong or unkind.

The other important thing is to be completely honest with yourself about your motives. Are you interacting with people to boost your self-image, to distract yourself from an unpleasant situation, or just because you're bored? There's nothing really wrong with any of those motivations, but try to remember that others may attribute vastly different motives to your behavior.

It's wonderful when dates go well and blossom into a relationship. You're happy, the object of your affection is (presumably) happy, so everyone you know should be happy, right? Oh, your friends probably are happy for you . . . unless, of course, your newfound relationship is the only thing occupying your thoughts and conversations. Or, even worse, if your newfound relationship is so all-encompassing that you've abandoned all other social interactions and given your friends the impression that you've dropped off the face of the planet. Don't shake your heads at the Lady of the Manners like that and say you'd never do such a thing; she's seen it happen *far* too many times before.

It's understandable why such behavior happens, of course. New infatuation, love, or lust is a powerful thing, and they make your brain chemicals go all hippity-skippity. It's not as if you really mean to ignore your friends or talk only about the object of your affection. And if your friends are honest with themselves, they've probably been guilty of the same behavior at one time or another. (The Lady of the Manners will take a brief moment here to reflect upon her younger self, cover her eyes, and mutter, "What was I *thinking?!*")

But try to be self-aware enough to realize that you need to spend time with people other than your beloved and that you absolutely need to find other topics of conversation, if for no other reason than you'll have new ideas and stories to share with your romantic partner. There are, of course, swarms of other important reasons not to cut yourself off from all other social interaction, such as the notion that your friends are just as important to your mental and emotional health as your beloved is, that ignoring everyone and everything when you have a new relationship is just a wee bit self-centered, and that making one person the focus of nearly everything you say and do isn't healthy.

"But why are you with *him/her*?!"

Many people believe that Goths should only become romantically involved with other Goths and that you shouldn't get involved with a person who doesn't share your every interest and match your wardrobe. But wait! Can a Goth find happiness in giving his or her heart to someone outside the spooky and black-clad throng?

Of course! There is no rule that Goths must date other Goths. The Goth Cabal (which *still* doesn't exist) has not issued any such statement and never will. Now, the Lady of the Manners understands why people might think that Goths shouldn't date (or marry) outside of the scene; after all, people are often attracted to others whose interests they share. But someone liking the exact same things you do is no guarantee of romantic happiness. The Lady of the Manners really does believe that relationships are stronger when each partner has interests outside the relationship. Maintaining a separate identity is not only healthier, but it also gives partners much more to talk about when they are together.

Another reason to date someone who is not a Goth is that there are those in our spooky little subculture who . . . how can the Lady of the Manners phrase this? Who believe the hype, who believe that you must be hard-core ooky-spooky Goth all the time. There is a difference between someone who believes that every day is Halloween and someone who thinks that sleeping in a bed instead of a coffin means you're not a Real Goth. The Lady of the Manners feels that anyone who constantly needs to proclaim his gothness with a capital "G" would not make a good romantic partner anyway and probably should be pitied, not dated. Why? Because anyone who needs to "name-drop" a personality trait or affiliation with a particular subculture is probably not . . . self-aware enough to be a good romantic partner. These people will be so wrapped up in trying to be the #1 spooksters in the graveyard that they may not have the time, energy, or emotional resources to play a true part in a relationship. In the Lady of the Manners's experience, these people are looking for an accessory to prove how spooky they are or someone who can add to their status in the Goth scene.

However, being involved with someone different from you is not without its challenges. There's the temptation to give your partner a gothy makeover. There's nothing wrong with that, of course, unless she really doesn't want to go out to the Goth club, doesn't feel comfortable wearing all black and eye makeup, doesn't want to watch Tim Burton movies over and over, or just don't feel that Goth is for her. And before you stomp your little stompy boots and wail, "But if he loved me, he'd change!" stop and think about how you might feel if the situation were reversed. What if your partner tried to make you over, change your appearance, or drag you along to things you weren't interested in all in an attempt to change you? That doesn't sound very enticing, does it?

Then, of course, there's the problem of not knowing whether your beloved is gently mocking your spooky little quirks in fond amusement or secretly thinks your inky-black wardrobe and Halloween-tinged outlook are ridiculous. If or when this particular specter of doubt starts rattling its chains, the Lady of the Manners suggests that you ask your beloved a direct question about your concerns. Very strongly suggests, as a matter of fact. There is nothing to be gained from trying to guess what is going on in your partner's head by analyzing his or her every reaction. That sort of behavior will accomplish nothing but driving you crazy. Occasionally you must ask your romantic partner if he's rolling his eyes at you in a loving, teasing manner, or waiting for you to "grow out of this phase." The first is perfectly fine and to be expected. (The Lady of the Manners herself has been known to ask her wonderful husband that question, usually after he sighs heavily upon finding her in the horror section of the used bookstore with her arms full of vampire novels.) The second reaction is one that should cause concern. As the Lady of the Manners pointed out just above, changing your partner to better suit you is not a particularly kind thing to do; however, waiting for your partner to grow out of a "phase" (be it hipster, punk, Goth, or any other subculture) goes a bit beyond unkind and hurtles straight down the path of resentment and heartbreak.

The Lady of the Manners is well aware that the "communication is important!" message has been covered by anyone who ever gave romantic advice in the history of time but does feel it needs to be repeated in this context too. If you don't feel you can ask the object of your affection these sorts of questions, what are you doing handing your heart over to her?

Of course, there's another side to the "But why are you with him/her?!" dilemma. Just what should one do if one detests the person with whom a dear friend is romantically involved?

Well, maybe "detests" is a little strong, but there is no getting around the fact that sometimes friends date people we don't like. Don't like, don't approve of, don't understand what our friends see in the companion . . . you get the picture.

So what to do? Well, there are a few paths to take, depending on how close the friendship is. If the person in question is a casual social acquaintance—someone you see only out at coffee or the clubs—then the Lady of the Manners is afraid you don't really get to say anything. You're more than allowed to huddle in a corner with close friends and (quietly, oh so quietly) exclaim, "What does she see in him?!," but as to marching up to your acquaintance and saying, "By the way, your taste in romantic partners is appalling and you need to have your head examined," no. Not even if the horrible partner in question repeatedly sticks his foot in his mouth, shows no social skills, or wears white undergarments under sheer black clothing and insists on dancing under the black lights.

What if your acquaintance (basking in the glow of new love or something else) asks you what you think of the horrible partner? This is when you fall back on one of those tried and true clichéd phrases such as, "I hope she makes you very happy." Keep in mind that you must say this with as much sincerity and enthusiasm as you can muster; no droning it out flatly or rolling your eyes, please. That could be just as offensive as telling your friend what you really think.

But what happens if one of your nearest and dearest friends is involved with a horrible partner? (As an aside: when the Lady of the Manners says "horrible partner," she does *not* mean someone who is violent or abusive. If someone you care about is involved with that sort, then you need to urge your friend to reconsider, but you shouldn't expect your friend to listen to you. Sad but true.)

When someone you hold dear shows . . . dubious taste in romantic partners, it's depressing. "But you're so funny! So smart, so attractive! What are you doing with *him/her*?!" will run through your mind often, which is to be expected. Just don't actually say it to your friend. Yes, the Lady of the Manners is serious. Sometimes the best option is not to say anything and just bide your time. Perhaps on the day you were introduced, you or the horrible partner were having an off day. You never can tell, so just be patient and wait.

But what if time goes by and you become convinced your friend is dating a dud, that the horrible partner's horribleness can't be explained away by an off day? Now do you get to shake your friend and tell her she can do better?

No, you still don't. You also don't get to direct subtle (or not-so-subtle) insults at the person your friend is dating. You must try to be as polite as you can manage. Of course, your friend may notice that your interactions with his or her "twoo wuv" are a bit strained and ask you why. At this point, you should probably say something along the lines of, "I know ——— makes you happy; we've just never hit it off," and then speak no more upon the matter, no matter how much your friend badgers you.

That's how it works in a perfect world, at least. How does it usually work in the real world? You still shouldn't try to shake some sense into your friend, but on those occasions when your friend and the horrible partner have quarreled, being the sympathetic ear and saying things like, "Are you sure you're happy with ———?" and "Remember when ——— did [insert last thing that annoyed your friend]?" If you and your friend are in the midst of an emotionally deep, soul-bearing conversation and you have a very, very strong friendship, then and only then should you voice your concerns about the romance. Even then, you should choose your words carefully and be prepared for your friend to completely ignore you, if you're lucky. If you're unlucky, your comments may lead to arguments and angry silences.

The Lady of the Manners realizes none of this is much fun. But honestly, there isn't a simple way around the subject. One last bit of advice about all this: If and/or when your friend breaks up with the awful person, don't gloat. Don't go on and on about how, "I never liked him, I never understood what you saw in him, he was horrible and not good for you." Just don't. Listen while your friend rants (if your friend is so inclined), be supportive, and then do your best to arrange a meeting with someone much nicer.

Goths and Valentine's Day

By all rights, Goths should adore Valentine's Day. Decadent meals by candlelight, red roses, exquisite little extravagances tied up with satin bows. You would think that Goths, with their fondness for romance and decadence, would be delighted with the holiday and spend ages figuring out just what dramatic gesture would best express their emotions to the objects of their affection. In fact, many Goths do indulge in that sort of thing. But other Goths, well, don't. And are very loudly bitter about it.

You see, most Goths were, at one point or another, social outcasts. They may not have had many friends, and they almost certainly were single on at least a few Valentine's holidays, which can lead to not just angst-filled poetry, but feeling rather spiteful about the whole notion of this holiday of candy hearts and flowers. In addition, some feel that the whole holiday is nothing but an exercise in crass commercialism and consumption and that any true sentiment one feels like expressing shouldn't be defined by greeting cards, heart-shaped balloons, and mass-produced stuffed animals clutching plush red hearts.

The Lady of the Manners, having spent her share of Valentine's Days single and bitter, does understand these views (and has long since ritually burned her horrible attempts at poetry). But the Lady of the Manners has developed a fondness for all the hullabaloo and frippery of Valentine's Day over the years. The more cynical amongst you may be sneering, "Well, that's because you're married!" but having a beloved partner isn't the only reason that the Lady of the Manners has come to appreciate the commercially hyped romantic holiday. When it comes right down to it, the Lady of the Manners is a romantic. Not just for herself and her dear husband, but for everyone. The Lady of the Manners wants people to have some sort of expressions of romance in their lives, and if the only way they're going to get them is via a box of chocolates and a bouquet of balloons every February 14, then so be it, and the Lady of the Manners will do her best to encourage it.

What does this have to do with other Goths? Oh, merely that the Lady of the Manners would like to implore them, no matter how gloomy they may be, not to set out to make others unhappy about the day of candy hearts and flowers. Do not respond to questions about your black clothing with statements such as, "I'm in mourning for love." Do not hiss or growl at any happy couples you may see. Do not rant at length about how tawdry the whole holiday is and that you are sickened by the emphasis on hollow gestures tied up with pink ribbons. By all means, seethe to your-self (and perhaps a few friends), but please don't try to crush the happiness of others beneath your stompy boots.

But wait! What if you are a Goth who *is* celebrating Valentine's Day? Well then, Snarklings, you should give in to your wildly ro-mantic impulses and create a memorable one. That doesn't mean bankrupting oneself, by the way. (Especially since certain romantic staples such as roses get bumped up in price to reflect the day.) No, a romantic gesture can be something as simple as a nicely written letter expressing your affection for your special someone. Or per-haps reading a chapter of a favorite book to your love. The Lady of the Manners is also fond of "traditional" gestures with a twist and thinks that a candlelit picnic (be it in a park, a graveyard, or even in someone's darkened apartment) is charming. (Yes, yes, the Lady of the Manners does consider all of those heart-shaped candies and knick-knacks modeled after the shape of a real human heart to be amongst those traditional gestures with a twist.)

Valentine's Day is also a great reason to host a special theme night at the local Goth club. Zombie proms, voodoo dolls and heart pin cushions, open mic nights with prizes for the worst, most bitter love-stricken poetry; all of these are events that even the most lovelorn and jaded Goths would flock to. Who knows? Perhaps you will meet someone who sparks your interest at a heartbreak-themed event and have happier Valentine's Days in the future.

Breakups, heartbreak, and mobbing the newly single

All Goths are romantics, even if they vehemently deny it. Then why does the majority of the subculture profess to take a cynical view of the whole dating, love, and romance whirl? Because Goths are all idealistic romantics at heart and either don't want to be ridiculed or have been hurt too often.

So there you are in love and suddenly everything changes. "I need some space." "I think we should just be friends." "It's not you, it's me." Or even, "I don't want to be involved with you," with no further explanation. After hearing one of these statements, there are some very important things to keep in mind.

Don't ask for an explanation from your now-ex beloved. You might think that sort of information will make you feel better, but it won't. Knowing the reason for the breakup won't change the sinking feeling that someone you cared for doesn't want you anymore, and no amount of "friendly" talks with your ex will expunge that feeling. Only time will do that. Besides, do you really want to be told, "Because I found someone else," "I'm bored," "I think you're a controlling, obsessive, abusive loony," or other statements of that ilk? No, the Lady of the Manners didn't think so.

Yes, cry. Listen to "your" song (or listen to "Pictures of You" by The Cure on endless repeat, which is pretty much a Goth breakup tradition), get maudlin, and stare blankly at your surroundings. This provides necessary catharsis.

But—try not to do it in public. Because this is the big trick to surviving a breakup; when in public (and especially when you might run into your ex-beloved or ex-beloved's friends), you need to seem like you're doing okay. Yes, this is duplicitous and runs counter to a lot of pop psychology theories that advocate honesty and show-ing your true feelings no matter where you are, but think about it for a minute. If you give full vent to your feelings of anger, despair, and weepiness no matter where you are, eventually you will lose the sympathy of people who just don't want to deal with your continual emotional drama.

This doesn't mean acting like you are perfectly happy and everything is won-derful. This means trying not to burst into fits of weeping or rage at the local club, out at a restau-rant, or at work. And the best reason for putting the effort into doing this? Word of how you're behaving will get back to your ex-beloved.

Imagine what will go through your former flame's mind; you seem to be okay with the breakup. Were you about to end the relationship anyway? Maybe you are secretly glad not to be involved any longer . . .

Thus, you've planted a worm of doubt in your former lover's mind, a nice, subtle piece of revenge for you. (The best revenge is to live a happy life after the breakup and go on to do things you want to. Trust the Lady of the Manners about this, for she knows of what she speaks.)

Do not turn up where you know your ex will be so you can show him how miserable you are. Do not torment yourself with, "What could I have done to make her stay?" Do not constantly ask mutual friends how your lost love is doing and if he is with someone else. Do not call and hang up when your ex answers, and for goodness' sake, do not send strange, stalker-esque letters, postcards, or e-mail. Even anonymously, even years after the breakup. Your ex may still figure out the mail is from you and just pity your inability to let go.

What if you're the person who initiated the breakup? Oh, there are some things you need to be aware of too; don't think you're getting away scot-free.

First, do the breaking up in person. No, breaking up with someone over the phone, via e-mail, LiveJournal, Facebook, MySpace, or in an instant message conversation is *not acceptable*. No, really. If you are ending a romantic entanglement, you owe the other person the courtesy of doing so face to face. The *only* reason for not doing so is if you are worried for your physical safety; even then, the Lady of the Manners suggests that you still have the breakup talk in person. But! Make sure the talk takes place in a well-lit public place and that you have a few friends nearby. (They should not, the Lady of the Manners must stress, be hovering over you as obvious backup, but do make sure your friends have a clear view of where you are and what is going on, just in case something goes very badly.)

After the first talk where you actually break up with the other person, don't give in to any impulses to talk things over. You're not helping, you're just making things more painful. Even if you mean the old cliché, "I want us to stay friends," leave your now-ex be-loved alone for a while. He needs time to get over the hurt and the understandable urge to scream and rant, if not throw objects, at you. If you run into your ex in public, be cordial and polite. Do not ask, "How are you doing?" She is miserable, it's your fault (even if you did it for the best of reasons), and she probably doesn't want to talk to you. Honor that feeling, and leave her alone.

As the person who broke things off, you don't get to make snide comments. No matter how silly or overly dramatic you think your ex-beloved is being, you don't get to make hurtful comments about it or grumble in the presence of anyone who might relay your feel-ings to your ex. Privately, you can cast aspersions on the behavior or mock new love interests, but publicly you have to be polite. Re-member, the ever-present gossip network in the Goth scene really *is* ever-present, and things have a way of being repeated to people you would rather not have hear them.

If you harbor doubts about whether you should have broken up with the person in the first place, don't mention them. You acted on your decision; let things lie for a bit before you go trying to re-open negotiations. If you were unsure about breaking up, you shouldn't have done it.

The Lady of the Manners is not going to say that there is a true love out there for everyone. Some people just aren't destined to live happily ever after with a partner. But that doesn't mean that they can't live happily ever after by themselves! That also doesn't mean you should stop trying or wall yourself off from the possibility of romance. When the Lady of the Manners thinks back over some of her more disastrous relationships, she doesn't regret them because eventually they led her to where she is today. Of course, the Lady of the Manners wishes that some of them weren't quite the horror stories they ended up being, but you live and learn. And in some cases, smile in a quietly superior manner when you run into a past love and realize you're better off. That's the end result you're aiming for.

The mobbing of the newly single in the Goth scene is something that the Lady of the Manners has seen happen time and time again. She's not sure what causes it since she knows that individuals are capable of chatting up someone they're attracted to without behaving as if their brains have dribbled out their ears, but as soon as someone in the Goth scene is newly freed from romantic attachments, the feeding frenzy starts. Guess what? The person at the center of the feeding frenzy is probably feeling very uncomfortable. While it's nice to feel wanted, and the ego-boost from the attention is a lovely thing, becoming the target of that sort of attention so soon after a breakup is disconcerting.

Not to mention it encourages the impression that members of the Goth scene have some sort of checklist of people to date, which isn't the most flattering reason to be flirted with. (The Lady of the Manners is sad to report she has even heard someone say, "Just put me on the list for when you get around to dating again," which has to be a new low in flirting.) If the object of your affection is newly single, it's best to take a restrained approach to flirting. And don't get all huffy if she doesn't even want to consider dating for a while. You may be a marvelous catch, but how can your crush possibly tell you apart from all the other people besieging her on all sides who firmly believe that *they* are marvelous catches? Don't spout any twaddle at the Lady of the Manners about needing to "strike while the iron is hot" or other such nonsense either. If you are genuinely interested in this newly single person, waiting until he feels comfortable with dating again shouldn't be a hardship. Chasing after someone the instant he becomes single does have a faint air of a short attention span to it, as if your affections might wander the instant the next glorious creature of the night becomes free of romantic entanglements.

Goth Weddings (both weddings for Goths and Goths attending "normal" weddings)

While Goths have weddings at all times of the year, October tends to be the month when gothy (and even non-gothy) couples get married. And before any of you start making offhand remarks about what a cliché it is, Goths getting married on Halloween, hee, hee, hee, oh, how spooky, etc., be aware you're chortling at the Lady of the Manners's own wedding anniversary, and it's no more of a cliché than other couples getting married in June (Midsummer anyone?). It really isn't—in fact, there isn't time of year for a wedding that doesn't have some sort of clichéd stigma. The Lady of the Manners is going to stop herself before she wanders down that tangent much further and get back to the topic at hand. Yes, there are weddings in October, gothy- and non-gothy-themed weddings, each of which has its own set of unique etiquette concerns.

Oh, look—your oh-so-spooky self has been invited to a wedding! By a couple who aren't gothy in the slightest but are still your friends. Of course you're going to attend, but there are just a few things you need to keep in mind:

Sure, you can wear black, but this is not the time to wear the PVC trousers or dress. Velvet, silk, a well-cut suit—anything that shows you put a little thought into your appearance but doesn't sartorially scream, "Hey! I'm a freak!" You also should avoid layers and layers of swirly eyeliner, overtly white face makeup, or black lipstick. Anything that's just a touch too dressy or gothic to wear to a job interview would be your best bet.

Relatives of the bride and groom will always come over to talk to you about how unusually you're dressed. Even if you think you aren't. Expect it to happen, and have some friendly and polite responses ready. That way, when great-grandma Smithers comes over to you and, in the tone of someone relaying an important secret, comments, "You're wearing black," don't stand there blinking in surprised irritation.

For that matter, be prepared to make polite chitchat with the other guests. You were invited because the couple wanted you there, so behave yourself out of respect for them. Don't bring up controversial subjects, don't get drunk because you're "so bored with these people," and don't think because you're the "token freak" that you need to act outrageously.

But wait! Morticia and Gomez are getting married, and you've been invited! No problem, it'll be just like a private party at a fabulous Goth club! Well, yes, kind of. Most wedding invites state a dress code: formal, black tie, dressy casual (which the Lady of the Manners feels is a mild form of cowardice—make the guests dress up!), costumes, and so on. If the invitation isn't clear, then ask the bride or groom. Who knows, maybe they'll answer, "Oh, we were hoping you'd wear that one outfit of yours . . ." and all your sartorial problems will be solved.

Now, even at super-gothy weddings, there will most likely be relatives who, while they love "the kids" and are happy to be attending the wedding, still don't quite get this whole black-clad, every-day-is-Halloween lifestyle. Don't tease them. Don't make fun of them, don't say things just to wind them up, and do not ignore them and pretend they don't exist. Answer any questions they may ask you in (again) a polite and friendly manner, even if they are questions or comments you've heard a billion times: "Are you a witch?" "So you think you're a vampire?" "Your hair is purple." "Is that your natural color?" "Do you dress like this all the time?" Do not roll your eyes or be condescending, even if you have heard it all before; the people asking you haven't, and they genuinely want to know. If they start asking you questions such as, "But why is she getting married in a red velvet dress?" or "Why are there bats on everything?" then tactfully suggest they ask the bride and groom.

What if you are the bride or groom, planning your Addams Family spooktacular wedding? It's your special day, darn it, and you should be allowed to do whatever makes you happy, right? Well . . . within reason. Are you paying for the wedding by yourself? If so, you're free to indulge every little black-glitter-embellished whim you can afford. If family members are helping with the costs, thank them profusely, pay even more attention to the budget, and do not try to wheedle more money out of them so you can do something even more elaborate.

Another thing to keep in mind is that while your respective immediate families may be used to your gothiness and won't even raise an eyebrow when you select a skeletal couple as a wedding cake topper, you still may have to have The Conversation with them. The Conversation might cover subjects such as "Yes, we do think purple, black, and silver are appropriate colors for our wedding," "No, we aren't going to ask Wednesday to dye her hair a 'natural' color for the wedding," "No, Grandma doesn't have to wear all black" . . . You get the idea. No matter how accepting your families are about the way you live your life, most parents (and grandparents, aunts, and uncles) have been secretly clinging to the idea that you will have a "normal" wedding—in a church, the bride in white, everything straight out of a wedding magazine. You have to let them down gently without upsetting them. If you're lucky, the family members in question will jokingly refer to their cherished little hopes themselves, with a comment that they always knew you'd do things in your own unique way.

Ultimately, weddings should be about two people making a

commitment to one another and celebrating that commitment with their loved ones. A big elaborate dress, a huge reception, eight velvet-clad bridesmaids—those are perks, and fun ones at that, but they aren't the important thing. If you (as someone planning the wedding or just attending) can keep that firmly in mind, everything should go smoothly.

SEVEN

Socializing, Cliques, and Gossip

Why being polite to people you don't like is important

A huge part of the Lady of the Manners's philosophy of life can be summed up in one simple sentence: You should strive to be polite to people, even if you don't like them.

Now the Lady of the Manners is sure there are swarms of you out there thinking, "Why? If I don't like someone, surely I'm allowed to snipe at her, make hurtful comments, and generally be cruel. Especially if she says or does things that I disagree with or think are stupid."

You aren't allowed to do that. Well, it isn't a case of "allowed" so much as "you shouldn't." The idea works something like this: if you can manage to be polite to people you think are blithering idiots, then being polite and charming to people you *do* like will be even easier.

You see, there are people in the "local scene" where the Lady of the Manners lives whom she would rather not talk to. In fact, if they suddenly moved away to an entirely different planet, the Lady of the Manners would probably dance happily about her living room. But when social situations conspire to throw the Lady of the Manners into contact with those people, does she tell them how annoying she finds them?

Standard Club Goth

Does she insult their beliefs, clothes, dancing styles? No, she does not. Mind you, the Lady of the Manners doesn't have a long involved conversation or spend a lot of time with them, but she tries very hard to not roll her eyes at them either. Remember, the Lady of the Manners is asking you to be *polite* to people you don't like, not to change your distaste for them. There is a wide difference between the two, and the Lady of the Manners suspects that not all of you are clear on it.

Being polite to people you dislike or don't get along with means that when you interact with them (be it in real life or online), you don't immediately snipe at something they say or do just because *they* are saying or doing it. For example, the Lady of the Manners has seen far too many instances of someone flaming or mocking another person for a comment and then turning around and agreeing with the very same comment from a different person.

Sometimes people you dislike have good ideas or less-than-obnoxious behaviors or generally redeemable qualities. You're just going to have to accept that, but it doesn't mean you have to be their best friend ever.

Being polite to people you dislike also means that when you have to interact with them, you don't "lead" the conversation to a topic you know will end with both of you shrieking at each other. The other person holds opinions that you know are wrong, wrong, wrong? That's nice, dear, but you still don't get to argue with your foe. It probably won't make you feel any better to know this person most assuredly feels the same way about you, will it?

Victorian
Goth

Now, the more alert of you will realize that not visiting topics of contention will lead to a whole lot of conversations about nothing, about the weather or other such boring things. Yes, you're right. The point here is that you probably shouldn't spend hours and hours talking to people you despise anyway, so make the conversations short and inoffensive, if that is at all possible.

Of course, sometimes it isn't possible. There will be times when you are forced to be with people you can't stand because you have mutual friends. This is where you *must* be polite. The Lady of the Manners can't stress this enough. What if the mutual friend has no idea that you would rather claw your own eyes out than spend time with so-and-so? A social gathering is not the time to demonstrate this by being beastly and unbearable, no matter how entertaining you personally may find it. For one thing, you don't want to make your friend uncomfortable; while you may think you're doing your friend a favor by demonstrating that the despised person is a complete twit, your friend will probably get mad at you for not playing nice with this guest. Do not make a scene, do not make snide comments, do not roll your eyes, and do not start an argument. Look at it this way—there is always a chance that the person you dislike didn't read this chapter and will be horrible and rude to you. That means, if you've managed to behave yourself, that you will come off looking like the better person. Ahhh, the moral high ground; it's a lovely place, isn't it?

However, Snarklings, at some point you will have to tell your friend that you don't share the same enthusiasm for the person you dislike. At which point your friend will probably ask for reasons why, leading into new treacherous territory. How much you

Deathrocker

confess is up to you, but do not mistake your friend's questions for a free pass to rattle off a list of everything you dislike about your foe. While the Lady of the Manners would like to think that a simple statement like, "I would just rather not spend time with ———," would be sufficient, she's pretty sure that you'll have to provide some explanation. You may discover that your friend wasn't aware of your feelings, and while he or she doesn't share them, your friend will offer to help you avoid awkward conversations.

Of course, you can always ask another mutual friend to act as a "buffer" between you and the despised person. Choose someone who will keep an eye out for run-ins and will rush over to provide silent (or not-so-silent) emotional support or give you a good excuse to politely and gracefully leave the conversation. However, having someone be your buffer can sometimes backfire if you become too reliant on the support. What if your buffer can't attend every social event you do? What if your buffer becomes annoyed or exasperated with you and decides to deliberately start awkward or inflammatory conversations involving you and the person you don't get along with? Not to mention that needing another person to be your support system when dealing with those you don't like strikes the Lady of the Manners as a trifle immature and insecure.

Really, the Lady of the Manners is completely serious about this. Some of her dearest friends socialize and spend time with other people that the Lady of the Manners cannot stand. But, those other people are important to the Lady of the Manners's friends, so she tries to tolerate them.

Oh yes, what is that you're saying? The Lady of the Manners isn't being honest about her feelings and opinions? Twaddle. Social conventions do not exist to help us be honest about our feelings. Social conventions exist to ensure civilized behavior so that people don't go trying to strangle each other over coffee. Once the person(s) you don't like has left the area, and if you *must* say something before your head explodes, hold whispered conversations with close friends about how much you don't like that so-and-so, how his views are suspect, how he has stupid shoes. Fine. Just don't give vent to those feelings publicly or start spreading gossip or other untruths about the person you don't like. And for heaven's sake, do *not* cause a scene. The Lady of the Manners doesn't have to tell you it's ridiculous to whisper behind your hand to your friends and then stop to stare at the poor creature you find objectionable, does she? Good, she was worried she might have to go into a long and drawn-out explanation.

Perkygoth

Why being circumspect about gossip and catty commentary is even *more* important

Rivethead

As much as it pains her to admit it, the Lady of the Manners has long since accepted the fact that Goth communities around the world run on gossip. Well, all of human social interaction runs on gossip, but the Lady of the Manners can only speak to how it works in her chosen subculture. Gossip, in its most basic incarnation, is merely news about people: who has a new job, who needs roommates, what happened at the party or club the other weekend. With the rise of online social networking sites and blogs, it's easy to stay in touch with friends across the world and feel like you are part of their lives. Of course, those same tools make it even easier for misinformation and rumors to spread like wildfire. If you think trying to set the story straight about what *really* happened last weekend is difficult amongst a group of people living in the same city, just try to explain what happened to people who weren't there and whose only knowledge may come from cryptic blog entries and possibly altered photos. There's no way to stop gossip either. And being extremely private and circumspect about everything you do will merely reduce the whispers and speculation and might even drive people to make up wild fictional rumors about you.

So if there's no way to keep people from gossiping, why is the Lady of the Manners suggesting that you try to avoid it? Because gossip can be hurtful and damaging to people, Snarklings. So when you're about to pass on the latest juicy rumor about someone, stop yourself and think about whether it's something that really needs to be repeated. The Lady of the Manners understands all too well the temptation of gossip, speculation, and catty commentary, especially when it comes to people you aren't terribly fond of and would like to see taken down a peg or two. But the Lady of the Manners also understands that finding out what . . . interesting . . . things people are saying about you is frequently an exercise in shocked mortification. Which is why she firmly believes that if you're going to gossip, you should indulge in it with as few people as possible and make it very clear which tidbits should not be repeated.

Cybergoth

Of course, the things that you don't want repeated probably will be repeated anyway, and there's a very good chance that the gossip will be passed along to its subject, who may confront someone about it. What should you do if you happen to be the person confronted about the gossip? The Lady of the Manners suggests that you show a bit of backbone and admit to being a gossipmonger. Yes, this means the subject of the speculation will probably be annoyed with you, and rightfully so. But not owning up to your actions is cowardly, and if you can't be strong enough to deal with difficult situations, then you shouldn't do things to cause them. Which, yes indeed, Snarklings, includes gossiping.

But what should you do if (well, when, really) you discover that you are the subject of a particular bit of gossip? There are a few options open to you:

 As the Lady of the Manners mentioned just a few scant paragraphs ago, you could trace the story back to whoever started it and confront this person about it. The good thing about this approach is that you will identify the most active gossiper in your circle. This can be helpful because talking to the lead gossipmonger can help clear up miscommunications. However, don't think that setting the story straight will cause the original rumor to wither away unnoticed, because it won't. But you'll be able to take some satisfaction in knowing that the truth is out there, even if not everyone will pay attention to it.

You could decide that you don't care what other people are saying. Yes, *ignore* the gossip. If you try to defend your behavior, the gossipers will gleefully assume they've made you upset and defensive. As to worrying about what the gossipers might tell new people, that's another exercise in frustration. The best you can do is hope that new people you meet have not already heard tales about you. If they have, there's nothing you can do about it except show that you're a delightful person to know. Just act like the gossip has no impact on your life.

Another way to limit gossip is to refrain from doing things that you would be ashamed of other people knowing about. This suggestion is a bit tricky because, as the Lady of the Manners has already pointed out, people will, in the absence of information, make up their own dratted stories about you.

Make up your own rumors about yourself, confess them in confidence to a select few people, and then wait to see how long it takes until they've spread throughout the social circle or scene you're part of. The Lady of the Manners is especially fond of this tactic because not only will it identify the biggest gossips, but it is always fun to see what sort of nonsense one can come up with that will be taken as gospel truth if prefaced with, "You can't tell anyone about this, but . . ." Not to mention that it's quite entertaining to find out just how embellished your fictitious rumor will be after it sneaks through the gossip chain.

Of course, no one wants to be known as a gossip. People may always want to talk to you, but they probably won't trust you very much. Is the thrill of being the person with all the dirt worth also being known as the person who can't keep a secret?

The difference between snarkiness and cattiness

To the unobservant and perhaps uninformed, there is no difference between snarkiness and cattiness. And on the surface, there are some similarities. Both types of commentary tend

Romantigoth

to be acid edged, and Goths are rather infamous for indulging in both. But there is a key difference between the two, and the Lady of the Manners sometimes worries that not enough Goths (or anyone else, for that matter) know the difference. Well-done snark, while sometimes wildly acidic, never should cross over into the territories of bitchy or mean. Catty comments, however, are almost always frosted with a heavy layer of bitchiness and frequently aimed straight at a person's weak spots. The problem is, of course, that the differences between snarky and catty can hinge on variables such as the tone of voice used in delivering said commentary, the relationship between the speaker and his or her target, the general personality and reputation of the speaker, and so on. For example, while the Lady of the Manners laughs in good-natured recognition when friends refer to her as an implausible and clothes-obsessed cartoon character, hearing that comment from someone the Lady of the Manners *isn't* friends with would sting a bit. (Well, probably not because the Lady of the Manners accepts and embraces her more lampoonable quirks, but you get the idea, Snarklings.)

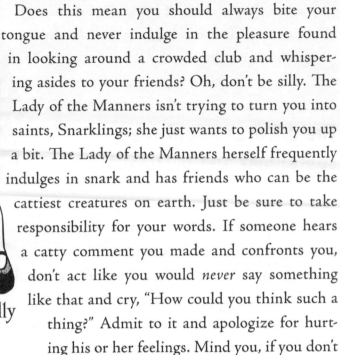

Gothabilly

Does this mean you should always bite your tongue and never indulge in the pleasure found in looking around a crowded club and whispering asides to your friends? Oh, don't be silly. The Lady of the Manners isn't trying to turn you into saints, Snarklings; she just wants to polish you up a bit. The Lady of the Manners herself frequently indulges in snark and has friends who can be the cattiest creatures on earth. Just be sure to take responsibility for your words. If someone hears a catty comment you made and confronts you, don't act like you would *never* say something like that and cry, "How could you think such a thing?" Admit to it and apologize for hurting his or her feelings. Mind you, if you don't feel any remorse about what you said, don't bother apologizing. However, understand that such behavior will eventually secure you a reputation as a catty bitch, no matter what your gender, and while that isn't the worst reputation to have, it does carry a subtext of "mean and unpleasant." In other words, don't be naive about what impact your comments may have.

The difference between self-confidence and self-absorption

Self-confidence is when you believe in yourself enough to go forth and become the person you want to be. Self-absorption is when you feel that everyone you talk to wants to be you or wants to hear about you and every thought you may ever have. Self-confidence is a wonderful thing and should be nurtured. Self-absorption is tedious to behold and should be avoided.

Self-absorption is where a lot of the negative clichés about Goth personality traits spring from. That we're all shallow, whiny, only care about shocking people, and prefer to be left alone to wallow in our woe in our darkened rooms. While mere silly twaddle, these negative clichés are pervasive and you need to be aware of them and be vigilant that you don't slide down into their grimy clutches.

Gothic Lolita

The difference between exclusivity and snobbishness

Goths have a bit of a reputation as elitist snobs. Some say we all stand around in gloomy clots, looking down our pale little noses at everyone else. There is the teensiest grain of truth to that reputation—we Goths do have a tendency to be a bit on the exclusionary side of things—not because we think we are *so much better* than everyone else, but because we're wary of what questions or comments may come our way. The Lady of the Manners wishes it wasn't so, but the sad truth of the matter is that most Goths have had to put up with bullying and unkindness from all sorts of people because they are different. So of course we're all a bit standoffish around people we aren't sure of. That's why there's such a thing as the freak nod of mutual recognition. Unacquainted Goths will usually subtly acknowledge one another when crossing paths because, though complete strangers, they're both still black-clad eccentrics and part of the extended tribe.

The Lady of the Manners can hear the question now, "But what about the people who are gothy on the inside, but don't look Goth?" Unfortunately, this is another source of the belief that Goths are

Goths frequently take pains to present themselves as they wish to be perceived and maintain their dark and shadowy aesthetic. Because that aesthetic tends toward the dramatic and theatrical, many Goths have adopted certain social niceties from past eras. The best example the Lady of the Manners can think of is that many Goth gentlemen are fond of kissing a lady's hand as a greeting. Which, in theory, is a delightful practice. In real life, it can be a delightful practice, or it can leave the lady discreetly trying to dry off her hand. Does that mean gothy gentlemen should refrain from politely raising a lady's hand to their lips? No, but the gesture should be just a quick brush of the lips, not a lingering or, erm, damp experience. (Yes, Snarklings, this means no licking a lady's hand. That sends a somewhat different message. If indeed you want to send that sort of message, be very sure that the recipient won't be—what's the word?—squicked by your saliva and unnerved by your forwardness.)

Other social niceties Goths have adopted are slight bows or curtsies accompanying a handshake (which the Lady of the Manners thinks is charming, if sometimes a touch pretentious), and honest to goodness handwritten thank you notes. (The Lady of the Manners is particularly fond of the idea of thank you notes but must sheepishly admit that she almost never manages to send them herself, due to her hectic, scatterbrained life. While she would love to encourage everyone to send graciously worded notes on black-edged cards, the Lady of the Manners isn't going to be cross with people who don't.)

snobs who assume that anyone who doesn't look like a Goth won't be sympathetic to the Goth mindset. Again, this defense mechanism stems from Goths' uncertainty about how strangers will treat them. But the Lady of the Manners is sad to say that she has heard that some Goths just can't be bothered to speak to anyone who they don't like. Which is ridiculous, in the Lady of the Manners's opinion, because Goths are quite willing to complain about how people unfairly judge *them* because they don't look like everyone else.

The Lady of the Manners would like to point out to her fellow Goths that limiting contact to other black-clad eccentric types seems like a clever way to surround oneself with like-minded individuals, but it's no guarantee. Though "variety is the spice of life" is indeed an oft-repeated cliché, it's also true. There's a big interesting world out there; excluding parts of it just because they don't fit your personal aesthetic preferences seems rather silly and limiting.

Subcultural crossovers and the blurring of boundaries

Subcultural crossovers? Whatever could the Lady of the Manners mean by that? Snarklings, haven't you noticed the cross-pollination between the Goth and Fetish subcultures? This is fine and dandy because the two subcultures share mutual points of interest: interesting or exotic clothes, some types of music, being regarded by outsiders as a trifle odd if and when you talk about your hobbies, and so on. But even with those things in common, there are still some issues that require sensitivity and tact from both camps. Luckily for all of you, the Lady of the Manners has come up with some guidelines for just those sorts of situations:

🦇 Don't automatically assume a person belongs to the same subculture as you do. Just because someone wears PVC, leather, or a corset does not mean he or she is kinky. A person who attends an event billed as a "fetish night" might be there merely for the music (or because it is a nonsmoking venue, or because a friend brought her along). If you want to involve someone in . . . extracurricular activities, *ask first*. If the person says, "No, thank you," smile and let it go. Gothy types also need to remember that black clothes are not exclusive to their own dark 'n' gloomy lifestyle. Not all people wearing black PVC trousers are Goths, but they're not all poseurs either.

🦇 Pay attention to the theme of events you attend. If you frequent the weekly "fetish night" at the local Goth club, don't complain about the half-naked people wandering around or the floggings. That's what "fetish night" means, you sillies. If you don't want to see that sort of thing, then you what sort of events you should avoid, don't you?

🦇 Contrariwise, the kinky folk in the Goth scene must also pay attention to what is going on at local clubs. If an event isn't a designated "play" night, then keep your private entertainment just that—private. If the mood strikes you and you feel the need for your particular type of release, leave the club and go somewhere more accommodating (and that doesn't mean the club restrooms). Yes, Goths are (supposedly) open-minded, but you shouldn't push your luck. Besides, you never can tell who might be at the club that night, and it would be a horrible thing if your personal activities led to some sort of legal unpleasantness. Appropriate behavior in appropriate places—that's the thing to remember.

🦇 It is the height of rudeness to take up part of the dance floor with a spanking or other fetish/kink scene. The dance floor is for just that—dancing. If you are at the sort of place that welcomes the fetish community, then it's likely there are specific places for fetish/kink play to take place. Goths tend to take up a lot of room dancing as it is, what with the flailing and the spinning and the outstretched arms and whatnot; don't encroach on their space any more than they already do with each other.

It is also rude to hang around gawking at people who are in the middle of a fetish scene. They aren't doing those things for your entertainment. (Usually. Some clubs do have special "fetish performances," but it will be fairly obvious when a scene calls for spectators.) A discreet glance now and then is fine, but don't stare. And especially don't offer commentary or advice—if the people involved want outside participation, they will ask for it.

Tolerance, tolerance, tolerance. Don't ask prying questions in a snotty tone of voice, don't say things like, "You're at a fetish club—why are you wearing so much clothing?" and certainly don't point at what you see and make scandalized exclamations. (Who would attend a fetish event and do something like that? People who are okay with the idea of the fetish scene in general but may not be ready for the real-life sight of a middle-aged man wearing nothing but clear plastic.) No matter how shocked you are by what you see, you must keep your composure. If you're really freaked out, leave. The Lady of the Manners does not mean that in a chastising manner either. Sometimes you can't tell if you're really, truly going to be okay with these sorts of things until you see them, and there is no shame in deciding you don't want to be around them. Shame comes in if you decide to start haranguing everyone around you to get them to stop what they're doing. Remember that old saying, "If you can't say something nice, don't say anything at all"? It holds true here. Just go home and do your scandalized exclaiming in private—that way you won't upset anyone and you can entertain your nearest and dearest with extended rants.

The flip side of this is that no one should feel pressured to "join in." Just because someone is a Goth doesn't mean he or she is part of the fetish scene or has to join it. This holds true for a lot of behaviors sometimes associated with the Goth scene that are not universal. "Goth" does not always mean "polyamorous," "bisexual," "into blood-drinking," "promiscuous," "plays role-playing games," or "really thinks he's/she's a vampire." Assuming that any of those things are true about people (even if they are black-clad weirdoes) is a bad move and will probably start an argument. When meeting someone for the first time, a pleasant way to start a conversation is to ask what they're interested in, so you have no call for making assumptions in the first place.

The Internet is not Real Life (with an aside about the Great Flounce-Off)

The Internet is not real life. Not by a long shot.

You would think, wouldn't you, that the Lady of the Manners wouldn't need to point that out, that it would be so blindingly obvious that no one would need reminding. Hah. What led the Lady of the Manners to the depressing realization that people needed to be reminded of this? A story recounted to her by a friend.

A friend of the Lady of the Manners (we'll call her LadySpooky) was out one evening at a local gothy club. LadySpooky thought she saw an acquaintance across the room and walked over to exchange pleasantries. As she was waving and saying, "Hi!" LadySpooky realized that this person wasn't who she thought. Being a polite girl, LadySpooky introduced herself and held out her hand. The other person, starting to extend his hand for a handshake, asked, "What's your board name?" (referring to the local online Goth community message board). "Oh, I'm not on the board," replied LadySpooky. This other person *pulled back his hand and walked away*.

(A small pause while the Lady of the Manners reins in her temper all over again.)

That, boys and girls, ladies and gentlemen, is inexcusable behavior. Just because someone isn't part of your particular slice of Internet life, that's no reason to snub his or her attempt at friendliness. At the very least, this person should have returned the handshake, introduced himself, and made up an excuse about having to go find someone before walking away.

Allow the Lady of the Manners to repeat herself. *The Internet is not real life.* There are billions of reasons people might not spend every waking minute online, including work, family, or having better things to do with their time.

"Better things to do with their time"—goodness, that's a fine thing coming from someone who spends an awful lot of her time online, isn't it? But the Lady of the Manners doesn't feel she's being hypocritical. Yes, there are all sorts of interesting things to be found on the Internet, and without it the worldwide Goth subculture wouldn't be anywhere near as strong or (in some cases) close-knit. But, like everything, the Internet is best in moderation. Is it vitally important that you associate only with people who post to the same boards as you? Or only people who have above X number of posts on those boards, have their pictures in the same web galleries, or are part of the same online social networking sites as you? No, it isn't. Sorry if the Lady of the Manners burst your little bubble there. In even just one year's time, someone else will be more active in the online Goth scene than you are, will have posted more pictures, and might just snub *you* for not being as Internet-fixated as they are.

Now, in addition to the idea that the Internet isn't real life, there's another concept the Lady of the Manners wants you to keep firmly in the front of your brain. When online, behave just like you're talking with those people face to face. It's very easy to forget there are real people with feelings, opinions, and reactions on the other side of your monitor—you're not just replying to a bunch of text on a screen. You shouldn't say things in e-mail (instant messenger, web forums, comments on people's journals, and so on) that you wouldn't say to the person's face. If everyone could manage this, the Internet would be a much, much better place.

The Lady of the Manners can already hear some of you sputtering, "But, but, I do try to do that! What about the people who respond with big stompy flames to everything I post?" Well, in the Lady of the Manners's worldview, those people are known as jerks. Remember, Snarklings, there will always be people who like to be rude, condescending, and unkind just because they think it's funny (or because they claim they only pick on the deserving, that they're just teasing, that the target overreacted, blah, blah, blah). If you end up dealing with someone like that, do not respond in kind—the Lady of the Manners begs you. It won't accomplish anything. You won't get an apology, you won't change the person's mind or behavior, and you'll merely get yourself all worked up over someone who doesn't deserve even a moment of your time. Ignore it. Don't rise to the bait of any inflammatory comments or posts; heck, don't even read any of these people's comments or posts if you can't wield that sort of self-control. The Lady of the Manners knows that it can be difficult. She occasionally gives in to overwhelming temptation herself, reads something by someone she knows will just annoy her, and then ends up walking away from the computer so she doesn't send a reply that will only start an argument. But half the battle is learning to recognize who is interested in having a discussion of differing opinions and who is just looking to start a fight. Avoid the latter as often as you can.

Of course, if you've spent any time at all on the Internet, you've encountered another particular strain of annoying and ridiculous behavior many times. (The Lady of the Manners fervently hopes you haven't indulged in it yourselves; if you have, don't spoil her illusions.) At some point, on every blog, message board, Live-Journal, MySpace page, or newsgroup, a version of the following will be posted:

"No one understands me / You are all SO MEAN / I am misunderstood! I am GOING TO LEAVE (delete journal / user profile / stomp off in a huff)!"

This sort of behavior is commonly referred to as *good-bye, cruel internets* or "I'm taking my toys and going home!"

Why is this a big deal? Because the person threatening to flounce off in a huff is trying to make other people feel bad about how they've been treating the flouncer. But one of the problems with pulling the Great Flounce-Off is that, well, it's a lot like the story of the boy who cried wolf. No one really believes that the person threatening to leave actually will. It's seen as a cheap ploy for attention, a cue for other people to exclaim, "No, no! We love you! Please don't go! You're obviously right about everything!"

Yes, that's a harsh interpretation. But it's an accurate one. And, to a degree, it works: people rush to reassure the flouncers that everyone *does* like them and would be shattered and bereft if they stopped posting their pearls of wisdom. But if the flouncers has any self-awareness at all, they might notice that the outpouring of adoration isn't as overwhelming as hoped, that it's almost as if some people didn't say anything at all. Of course, the people who resort to the *good-bye, cruel internets* ploys usually are not brimming with self-awareness, so they probably don't notice the lack of universal praise and just keep throwing these sorts of tantrums whenever they're upset or not getting their way.

Now, the Lady of the Manners is aware that some people who state that they are deleting their journals or leaving a message board or forum are *not* indulging in a dramatic reading of *good-bye, cruel internets* but actually intend to stop participating in that particular venue. But the difference in tone between the two styles is, at least to the Lady of the Manners, very obvious. People who have decided to move on usually say something like, "I've decided to focus my energies elsewhere," or "Things are getting busy for me and I don't have the time to keep up with this," whereas variations of the Great Flounce-Off include, "I don't think anyone understands what I'm trying to say, so I'm just going to stop posting," or "It's obvious that I'm making people upset or offending them, so I should stop posting." One of the tell-tale markers of the *good-bye, cruel internets* script is the flouncer's need for validation or reassurance.

So! In the hopes of stopping the flouncing-off epidemic that seems to be overtaking the Internet, the Lady of the Manners has some helpful suggestions:

Suggestion the First: If you realize that you've indulged in this sort of behavior in the past, *do not* repeat it. The Lady of the Manners is quite serious. If you catch yourself writing something that sounds even remotely like the *good-bye, cruel internets* script, stop and *do not post it*. Instead, ask a couple close friends for a sanity check and listen to what they say, even if it isn't what you want to hear. Be aware that while indulging in these sorts of posts might make you feel better in the short term, you will alienate other people and make yourself the object of bemused pity, if not outright scorn and ridicule.

Suggestion the Second: If you see someone performing the Great Flounce-Off, do not rush to console or reassure him or her. Ignore it. If the flouncer is a close friend, privately suggest that he or she stop throwing tantrums to get people's attention. How much tact you wish to employ is up to you; while the Lady of the Manners is always in favor of tact and diplomacy, sometimes you need to be blunt and say, "You're being an ass. Did you mean to be?"

Suggestion the Third: Sometimes *good-bye, cruel internets* can be worrying. If it sounds like the poster is contemplating self-harm, contact parents, a spouse, or close friends to pass on your worries. Yes, you might be overreacting, but the Lady of the Manners feels it is better to take this kind of post seriously and be wrong than to ignore it and live with a tragic outcome. If the poster gets angry with you for interfering, point out that he or she should choose words more carefully.

Why polite honesty doesn't always have the hoped-for effect

Polite honesty is indeed a habit to aspire to. Sadly, there is a wide gulf between polite honesty and stating one's opinions with no regard for other people. And some people's definitions of polite honest behavior change when *they* are on the receiving end of it.

In the Lady of the Manners's universe (which features a lovely, if strict, dress code), polite honesty means expressing your opinion truthfully, calmly, and without the hidden (or not-so-hidden) agenda of starting an argument. (The Lady of the Manners trusts that all of you know the difference between a discussion and an argument. Don't laugh; just let her cherish that illusion for a bit longer, please.) Polite honesty means there are no overtones of "You're an imbecile if you don't agree with me" and no insults thinly disguised as advice for someone's own good.

If the Lady of the Manners may be so bold, she'd like to suggest that all of you go back and reread that last sentence, because the Lady of the Manners feels that's where the whole idea of polite honesty breaks down. The Lady of the Manners has witnessed far too many instances of "cruel to be kind" that seem to be missing the "kind" part of the equation. Also, even if someone has no social skills and causes fights every time he opens his mouth (or sits down in front of a computer), there is no good way to tell him that without it going badly. It doesn't matter how much he may need someone to (very politely) tell him these things; just because he needs to hear it doesn't mean he'll listen.

The few times the Lady of the Manners has decided to be politely honest with someone concerning uncomfortable truths, the Lady of the Manners approached the conversation knowing that this person probably would not listen, might say hurtful things in return, and probably would take her actions as a personal attack. The Lady of the Manners cannot think of anyone, herself included, who could take that sort of critique without becoming very prickly and defensive.

Does all this mean that the Lady of the Manners thinks everyone should abandon the notion of polite honesty? Good heavens, no. The Lady of the Manners just wants people to be aware that no matter how good your intentions, odds are high that the object of your criticism will become cranky. It's possible you might be pleasantly surprised, but don't bet your collection of pointy boots on that chance. If someone asks your opinion on a potentially sensitive or difficult subject, make sure she really *wants* your opinion, and is not merely looking for reassurance or agreement.

But what should you do if someone really does need to hear some uncomfortable truths? First, think very hard about whether or not your heart-to-heart will make any difference. The Lady of the Manners wouldn't dream of having this sort of conversations with certain people, mostly because she is well-aware that those people wouldn't listen to a blessed thing the Lady of the Manners had to say. There is a vast difference between having a difficult conversation and shouting into the abyss, and the Lady of the Manners wouldn't wish the latter on anyone.

Second, try to determine what you are going to say *before* you start the conversation. Well before. If you know what you want to say and how you are going to say it, you might be able to keep the conversation from turning into a heated argument.

Third, keep in mind that whomever you're speaking with will probably feel attacked or hurt, no matter how mild you think you're being. This person may not flounce off in a huff or start yelling but probably will still feel a little touchy. You may need to repeatedly explain that your intention was not to cause distress but to express something that needed to be said.

If, after keeping all of those things in mind, you still are determined to pursue the difficult but politely honest conversation, the Lady of the Manners wishes you luck and hopes that not too many inter-scene dramas flare up as a result.

EIGHT

Fashion: One of the Great Goth Obsessions

The never-ending debate about fashion vs. music (part 1)

"Goth is really about fashion. Anyone can listen to the music, but if you're a Real Goth, you look like one." This statement sums up one side of the great Goth argument that is always going on somewhere. It's an argument that, in addition to being never-ending, gets very heated and tends to feature both sides flinging around the withering epitaph "poseur." The argument can be summed up thusly: The driving force behind the Goth subculture is ——, and that blank is filled with either fashion or music. The idea that both are equally important to the world of Goth is, while a charming notion, not a widely championed one.

"Waitaminute!" the Lady of the Manners can imagine you saying. "But didn't Goth come from the punk music scene? Doesn't that mean music is the obvious answer?" Well, no, not really. While Goth did creep forth from the shadow of punk, the look was there from the beginning. The wildly tousled and unnaturally colored hair, the thick eyeliner, the lace and shredded fishnets. For many people, the ritual of getting all gothed up to go out to a club was more important than listening to music at the club itself. Sure, nightclubs and concerts provide gathering places for the spooky tribes, but the attire lets you identify (to a degree) who else may

be part of that tribe. If you say "Goth" to someone outside of the subculture, they probably don't automatically think of iconic Goth bands such as Bauhaus, Siouxsie and the Banshees, or The Sisters of Mercy. No, the non-Goth probably thinks of someone with unnaturally or cosmetically enhanced white skin, and hair, eyeliner, and clothing of a uniform midnight shade. In other words, there are all sorts of people who may like a selection of various Goth songs but would never be identified as such because of the lack of visible subcultural markers. Whereas if someone merely flirts with an all-black outfit and darker-than-the-norm eye makeup, people fall over themselves in the haste to affix the Goth label.

Most days, the Lady of the Manners comes down on the side of fashion in this long-standing debate. (See the chapter on music for further explanation of why she wavers between the two sides.) It takes dedication to bring your closet over to the dark side, especially if you want to do more than merely wear black jeans and a T-shirt with an appropriately spooky slogan. Thanks to the magic of the Internet, it is easier than it was in the days of yore to collect a closet full of gothy finery, but sporting a full-on Goth look still takes a smidge more effort than accumulating a music playlist tinged with darkness. (Ooooh, the Lady of the Manners can just imagine the glares she's getting from some people for that statement! Just wait Snarklings, and read on.)

Appropriate attire suggestions for job interviews, the corporate world, family get-togethers, the summer heat, the chill of winter, and other events

So you've decided to turn your closet into a shadowy realm. But then perhaps it occurs to you that your new wardrobe of darkness, while decadent and striking, might not be the most appropriate garb for certain occasions. Should you wear a velvet frock coat and frilly shirt to a job interview? What about to work? The answer to those sorts of questions is, well, maybe. "Maybe," because you don't want to completely disguise who you are when interviewing for a job. Try to look like yourself, but dress a bit more formally, a bit more "businesslike." A black suit jacket worn with a dark red or purple shirt will keep you from looking like an undertaker but will hint that your personal style is not quite that of the average interviewee. If you are intent on working in a field where vibrantly colored hair is frowned upon, accept that fact and don't contemplate dying your hair blue.

For that matter, be aware of the corporate culture in the field you're looking to join, and use that knowledge to inform your choices for interview-wear. The Lady of the Manners works in the software industry, which has a somewhat elastic dress code, to say the least! So while the Lady of the Manners has worn severe frock coats and petticoat-enhanced skirts to job interviews, she knows that not everyone will be able to do that.

The Lady of the Manners doesn't have to tell you that your success in the corporate world is largely due to the quality of your work, does she? Being pleasant and polite to your coworkers is important, but being a clear communicator and doing your job well is even more so. The Lady of the Manners is quite serious, you know. Being good at what you do is vastly more impressive to managers than looking like everyone else. As you build up an employment history, remember that in most industries, your skills and knowledge are far more important than how you look. Yes, it's absolutely vital to make a good impression, which does mean that you shouldn't wear PVC trousers and a T-shirt with a semi-naked vampire lady on it to a job interview. (You weren't going to do that, were you? The Lady of the Manners is sure you wouldn't have but does sometimes worry.)

If you're a Goth in the corporate world, don't feel you must be wary and defensive, that your coworkers wouldn't understand you, that you have to hide your gothness or tone down your personality. But keep in mind that your dark and possibly morbid sense of humor may, at first, be a little unsettling for coworkers. When your coworkers ask about your wardrobe or desk decor, don't roll your eyes at them or act annoyed at their questions, even if they are the same questions that you've heard countless times from other people.

Setting aside the fact that it's not your coworkers' fault that you've been asked, "So what's with all the black clothes?" a bazillion times before, there's that little fact that treating one's work colleagues politely is vastly important. Office politics, while considered a cliché, are a fact of life. While the Lady of the Manners is certain there will be times when you want to unleash your iciest tone and most withering glare upon a coworker, those things can be *career-limiting moves*. Yes, even when it's done in response to a coworker asking you if you think you're a vampire. The other side to this, of course, is to have a sense of humor about the whole

"Goth at the office" lark. The Lady of the Manners's coworkers are fond of having her stand (well, loom, as much as she's able at 5'4") in the doorway of a room where a meeting is running late. Eventually someone notices the black-clad Goth lady in the doorway, does a double-take, and realizes that perhaps it's time to wrap up the meeting so the next group of workers can take over the space.

Finally, try to keep in mind that many non-Goths think that Goth is a phase, something in which people dabble in their teens and early twenties but set aside when it's time to join the "real world" as an adult. The thing is (as the Lady of the Manners has mentioned), that is not actually the case. Many CorpGoths, sometimes mistaken by their coworkers for just-out-of-college youngsters, have years of experience and skills in their chosen field. Their less-than-corporate appearance doesn't mean they don't understand how "things are in the real world"; instead, they're secure enough in their skills and in who they are that they don't feel the need to adopt any protective coloration as camouflage.

In a perfect world, family get-togethers would have nothing in common with job interviews; your family would accept and welcome you warmly no matter what you look like. But even if you are one of the lucky ones with such a family (as is the Lady of the Manners, thank goodness), there are still scenarios involving relatives that require you to put a little more care and thought into your appearance.

The most important thing to remember is to be respectful. If your grandparents or your great-aunt Esmerelda are of a more . . . conservative mindset, do not set out to deliberately antagonize them with your apparel. You don't have to disguise yourself as a run-of-the-mill normal person, but don't wear that shirt with "fuck" printed repeatedly across it. Don't wear anything too reminiscent of what you'd wear out to the Goth club; club clothes tend to be a little too provocative or risqué for family gatherings. If you are a Goth whose style tends toward the more antique end of the spectrum of black, you will have an easier time garbing yourself for a family party than one of the more deathrock or fetish-style Goths. Silks and velvets tend to raise fewer familial eyebrows than, say, ripped fishnets and a vinyl corset.

You may be thinking, "But I'm expressing myself!" Yes, Snarklings, and the Lady of the Manners wants you to do that. But sometimes expressing yourself in a slightly quieter sartorial tone will keep a family gathering from turning into hours of disapproving looks and lectures.

Summer

Again, in that perfect world, if the Lady of the Manners had her way, the weather would be perpetually autumnal. Yes, yes, the changing of the seasons is a lovely thing (and is absolutely necessary; the Lady of the Manners is not completely oblivious to that fact), but let's face it, the usual Goth wardrobe is not ideal for all weather conditions. Summer is the obvious problem season for Goths; not only does all-black clothing absorb the heat *very* efficiently, but it's hard to maintain an air of otherworldliness and mystery when you're a peeling, sunburned mess. You will need to develop some strategies for coping with the heat and the sun. Wear loose, billowy clothing in white, ivory, or pale grey. You can wear loose, billowy clothing in all black (heaven knows the Lady of the Manners doesn't give up her black dresses during the summer), but just understand that a lighter color will better deflect the heat. Try to not to wear head-to-toe PVC or polyester. (You can, if you really want to, but then you probably shouldn't complain about being too warm. You brought it on yourself.) Summer is an excellent time to scamper around in lightweight bloomers, chemises, and petticoats. Yes, the Lady of the Manners realizes this suggestion isn't of much use to her gentlemen read-ers. Perhaps shirts and trousers made from lightweight cotton or linen? And though the Lady of the Manners knows it's a hardship, you really should try to forgo stompy boots and in-stead find sandals or black canvas sneakers.

But Goths of all genders should carry a parasol; not only will you look delightfully antique, but you'll have shade with you wherever you are. Parasols can be as simple as a Chinese-style paper parasol (easily found at all sorts of stores and various online retailers) or as elaborate as a lace-frilled vintage confection. How-ever, the easiest way to add a parasol to your wardrobe is to find an umbrella you like (thrift stores are wonderful for this) and decorate it to your heart's content. You can paint designs on it, sew (or hot-glue) lace ruffles, silk roses, or feathers around the edge, or wrap the handle in ribbons and tassels. These same embellishments can be made to any wide-brimmed hat you happen to find on your thrifting expeditions, turning a plain (black) hat into something worthy of an Edward Gorey illustration.

Other than adjusting your attire for the weather, try carrying a folding fan to make your own cooling breeze, coat yourself in a good,

---

What are the basic cosmetic products no makeup-enthralled Goth should be without? The following is a list of what the Lady of the Manners considers essentials, along with some recommendations for the Lady of the Manners's favorite products. But! Be an informed consumer: seek out and read reviews of products, and don't be afraid to ask sales clerks at department stores if they have samples of the products available for you to try.

Sunblock, one that is at least SPF15 and protects against both UVA and UVB. You want one that spreads easily and is non-greasy. The Lady of the Manners favors Neutrogena's Ultra Sheer Dry-Touch sunblock in SPF 70 or 85. And yes, she wears it every day, even in winter.

A good moisturizer to nourish and protect your skin. What works for one person's skin may be a greasy disaster for another, but the Lady of the Manners applies Skin Food by Weleda every night after washing off her makeup.

Concealer, for hiding blemishes and dark circles under the eyes. The Lady of the Manners's absolute favorite concealer is the ridiculously pricy Touche Èclat by Yves St. Laurent, a product she refers to as "sleep in a clicky-tube."

Translucent powder. There are all sorts out there, in both loose and pressed formats. Translucent powder is good for "setting" your makeup and helping control shiny patches. The Lady of the Manners is very fond of Aromaleigh's Ultra Resolution Finishing Powder for loose powder and Urban Decay's De-Slick Mattifying Powder for a compact to carry around.

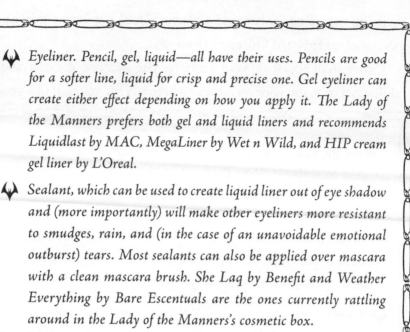

- Eyeliner. Pencil, gel, liquid—all have their uses. Pencils are good for a softer line, liquid for crisp and precise one. Gel eyeliner can create either effect depending on how you apply it. The Lady of the Manners prefers both gel and liquid liners and recommends Liquidlast by MAC, MegaLiner by Wet n Wild, and HIP cream gel liner by L'Oreal.

- Sealant, which can be used to create liquid liner out of eye shadow and (more importantly) will make other eyeliners more resistant to smudges, rain, and (in the case of an unavoidable emotional outburst) tears. Most sealants can also be applied over mascara with a clean mascara brush. She Laq by Benefit and Weather Everything by Bare Escentuals are the ones currently rattling around in the Lady of the Manners's cosmetic box.

- Mascara, partially because eyeliner without mascara looks unfinished and half done. The Lady of the Manners isn't going to give you a mascara recommendation because it seems like she's constantly trying new formulas.

- Lipstick, lip balm, or lip gloss. Something to keep your lips moisturized, and (if you prefer) colored. The Lady of the Manners has been on a quest for the perfect deep pomegranate wine lipstick for what seems like all of her life and currently is switching between colors by MAC, Besame, Wet n Wild, and NARS.

- Makeup remover. Oh, Snarklings, don't go to bed wearing your makeup. Just don't. In a pinch, baby wipes will remove everything and be kind to your skin.

high SPF sunblock (including your ears, the back of your neck, and any other exposed skin), and be sure to drink plenty of water.

Now, on to makeup. Summer can do terrible things to most gothy makeup styles. Foundation gets caked and streaky, care-

fully applied eyeliner can smudge and run, and mascara can melt right off into unbecoming spots. The obvious solution is to take a "less is more" approach; instead of a full face of foundation, apply only concealer where it's needed and use a light dusting of translucent powder. Try switching to waterproof eyeliner and mascara, or find a cosmetic sealer to apply over your usual brands, which will render them smudge-proof.

When the Lady of the Manners rules the universe, she fully intends to preserve glorious sunny days (all the better for picnics, tea parties, and croquet games), but she will never allow the temperature to rise above seventy degrees.

Winter

Of course, the black-velvet-clad masses face winter-specific problems too. Some of the footwear favored by Goths can't exactly be described as practical; the Lady of the Manners will never forget the first time she discovered that her beloved pointy-toe, multi-buckle boots had no traction whatsoever by sliding instead of strolling down a hill. Then there are pesky facts like almost all velvet doesn't deal well with rain and snow; long skirts can become quite hazardous when wrapped around your legs by the wind; and an all-black wardrobe can put your life at risk when you walk in the winter gloom after the sun sets. (Yes, an all-black outfit would probably show up quite well against pristine white snow, but the Lady of the Manners still has her doubts about its practicality on a dark winter's night when visibility is limited.)

So what is the fashionable Goth to do? Give up attractive footwear and scurry around in hiking boots and Gore-Tex? Of course not! Perish the thought.

First, find a good winter coat. Notice that the Lady of the Manners said *coat*, not *cloak*. While the Lady of the Manners is as fond of sumptuous velvet cloaks as the next Goth, cloaks are not really practical for most winter weather. They blow open in the wind (in a lovely and dramatic manner, true); they can get caught in car, train, or bus doors; and carrying any sort of bag other than a tiny handbag while wearing a cloak looks . . . silly. (The Lady of the Manners trusts that she does not need to point out the ridiculousness of wearing a backpack *and* a cloak at the same time.)

Look for a coat that can be closed securely (be it by buttons, zippers, or buckles), that is warm (be sure to take your usual local weather into account), and that will survive rainstorms (or sleet, snow, howling winds) without damage to the fabric. An attractive coat can indeed be found for just about every budget, but always remember to check thrift stores, consignment shops, and discount stores. If you're very clever and organized, you could remember to look for a good winter coat at yard sales during the summer. It's amazing what sort of bargains can be found on winter clothing during summer sales.

Winter is the time of year for boots, and not the ones with the four-inch spike heels. This is where those who are of the more industrial persuasion have it easier than the NeoVictorian and Romantic Goths; stompy boots are probably a skosh more practical than velvet granny boots. However, the Lady of the Manners hasn't given up all of her Victorian-style boots for ones with giant foam soles; instead the Lady of the Manners took her boots to the local shoe repair place and had thin rubber traction soles applied to them. The cost of having that done is far less expensive than buying new boots and helps your boots last longer. Now the Lady of the Manners scoffs at steep and possibly icy hills, instead of sliding precariously down them.

Layers. Layers, layers, layers. All sorts of thin thermal clothing items come in black, and some even have lace trim. Thin silk gloves not only look elegant, but they can be used as glove liners when the weather becomes truly icy. You can add and remove layers as weather and circumstances dictate. Also, one does not need to expose vast expanses of skin to dress in a Gothic manner, even when going to a nightclub. It's difficult to look mysterious and alluring if one's teeth are chattering from the cold.

If you're a pedestrian out and about after night falls, you should carry a small flashlight or blinky light with you so that you can make your presence known on the roads in any weather. An almost entirely black wardrobe is indeed one of the signs of being a Goth, but it isn't worth getting hit by a car for. The Lady of the Manners isn't suggesting that everyone sew light-reflective patches onto their clothing (the Lady of the Manners will leave that to the cybergoths), but the Lady of the Manners does think it's very important to make sure you are visible when walking after dark.

Keep in mind that some fabrics are not suitable for winter

weather. The Lady of the Manners realizes it's probably a bit harsh to hold that a person who exposes silk velvet to rain probably shouldn't be allowed to own anything made from that fabric ever again, but the Lady of the Manners still can't shake that (cranky) conviction. Weather can change unexpectedly, and once velvet becomes water-spotted, there are very few ways to fix it. One, of course, involves a needle board, steam, and trying to fluff the velvet back into a non-crumpled state. The Lady of the Manners, living in a somewhat damp climate, has instead resorted to turning the water-spotted fabric into lovely crushed velvet, which can be done by spending an afternoon scrunching up the item in question, spraying it with water, and then deliberately creating masses of wrinkles with a steam iron.

Winter weather can do unpleasant things to your skin and carefully applied cosmetics. Make sure to gently wash your face and apply moisturizer (and lotion, lip balm, or whatever skin care products you feel you can't live without). If you wear makeup, be sure to carry a mirror and any items you might need to repair things if your makeup runs due to rain or snow, or start wearing waterproof or long-wearing eyeliner and mascara.

Dress codes (both spoken and unspoken)

So how do you dress in a way that proclaims your dark aesthetic when you're shackled by a dress code? More and more schools are enforcing dress codes in the hopes of stopping bullying and violence, and in the hopes of quashing the trend toward skimpier and skimpier clothes for kids, tweens, and teens. (The Lady of the Manners likes to consider herself open-minded and not a fuddy-duddy, but *really*, Snarklings. The Lady of the Manners has, at times, been horrified to discover herself muttering, "Do your parents know you're dressed like that?!" in a scandalized tone.) Anyway, dress codes are becoming a common fact of life; what's a poor Goth to do?

Striped or spookily patterned socks or tights; a handful of pins or brooches on the lapel of a jacket or the collar of a sweater; clip-in hair streaks that allow you to dabble in eccentric and exciting hair colors without breaking the rules; these are some strategies for letting flashes of your true self peek out from the strictures of a dress code.

But what if all of those things are forbidden by the dress code you must follow? What if your place of employment, school, or parents

An aside to the younger readers: While the Lady of the Manners and others have made slightly disparaging comments about "mallgoths," there is nothing to be ashamed of if the only place where you can go to cast off the bland uniform and get all dressed up is the mall. There are not a lot of places for younger Goths to congregate, and parents seem to think their kids are less likely to get into or attract trouble at a shopping mall. The Lady of the Manners doesn't quite understand this thinking herself but knows it's fairly commonplace. The Lady of the Manners hopes that her younger readers will keep in mind that having a healthy sense of humor is even more vital when you're forced into exemplifying the mallgoth cliché. By all means, revel in your dark finery. Just realize that you're going to look even more outlandish and out of place than you might expect, and that no one looks spooky or cool, no matter how darkly regal or frighteningly rebellious they think they are, while loitering around the food court.

have made it quite clear that you cannot indulge in the dark and quirky tendencies of your inner self? Sadly, there isn't much you can do in those instances. The Lady of the Manners is well-aware of how bitter that news is, but sometimes there aren't any clever ways around rules or restrictions. You will have to grit your teeth, put on the bland uniform, and make plans for those times when you *are* able to dress in the manner you prefer.

The Lady of the Manners is about to let you in on one of the secrets of the Goth world, a secret that has thwarted people exploring the Goth subculture for years and years. Are you ready?

The secret is this: When attempting the Goth look, it isn't enough to throw on some black clothes and smudgy black eyeliner. There is indeed an unspoken dress code in the Goth world—a dress code that is subtler than just "wear black and look spooky." If that were the case, then those "Gothic Cheerleader," "Vampire Lord," and other Goth-themed costumes available every Halloween wouldn't be quite so cheesy, would they?

So just what does this unspoken dress code of Goth entail? Well, there was a hint in the preceding paragraph: the word *costume*. When someone compliments you on your "costume," it's a bit galling because, while the compliment is probably sincerely meant, "costume" implies you're indulging in a bit of fantasy, wearing an outfit from a play or another work of fiction. Your Goth wardrobe should not look like a costume, and it especially should not look like a costume you can buy in a plastic bag at a Halloween superstore.

Allow the Lady of the Manners to veer off on a brief tangent, Snarklings. The Lady of the Manners is both bemused and horrified by the proliferation of "Goth"-branded Halloween costumes and accessories.

One the one hand, these costumes look suspiciously similar to outfits she sees on Goths all the time. The only real difference is that the Halloween shop costumes are made from materials of somewhat dubious quality. Please, please, please consider the quality of materials and workmanship in the clothes you choose to wear day to day.

On the other hand, not only is the Lady of the Manners just a smidge tired of people asking where she bought her costume, but the Lady of the Manners also feels that "Goth" Halloween costumes just add to the perception problem under which the subculture already labors.

> Beware panne velvet, Snarklings. It never looks as sumptuous and elegant as you might want it to, no matter what other fabrics you pair it with. Also, beware retailers or eBay sellers who describe a garment as made from "penne." That is not a fabric; that is a type of pasta. If the seller can't get that fact right, what else might he or she get wrong?

None of the costumes really exemplify the dark romance, elegance, and whimsy that are vital aspects of the Goth subculture. Instead, they focus more on the "possibly dangerous freaks who think they're vampires, devil-worshippers, or sexual deviants" theme. But does this keep the Lady of the Manners from checking out the Halloween superstores to see what sort of bat-festooned goodies may be awaiting her there? No, it does not. The Lady of the Manners is a big fan of taking bits and pieces from many sources and reassembling them into something interesting. If some of those bits and pieces started life as costume accessories, well, that just gives things a post-modern flair, doesn't it?

What to do when people ask you why you're dressed like that

The Lady of the Manners has mentioned this in previous chapters but is just going to be blunt about it now. If you have decided to dress in a manner different from the norm, you *must* accept that people are going to stare at you and ask questions. Not only is that part of human nature, but ranting and railing about people looking at you funny when you are stalking about dressed as a creature of the night is ridiculous. You chose to dress that way, which means you don't get to complain about the attention your appearance garners.

Now, with that somewhat harsh opening out of the way, the Lady of the Manners does understand how important it is to be able to dress the way you want to, and that the majority of us Goths dress up because that's the way we want to look, not because we're seeking attention. The Lady of the Manners's daily wardrobe includes petticoats and a top hat, so she completely understands how annoying it is to be asked continually, "Who are you supposed to be?" or, "Are you in a play?" and other well-meaning yet clueless questions. However (and you knew there was going to be a "however," don't fib), even though the Lady of the Manners and all of you have been assailed by those sorts of questions over and over and over, the people asking don't know that. They're curious enough to ask you about it, so you should make the effort to respond politely. You don't have to act as if you've never been asked about your appearance before, but try to hide any exasperation or weariness you may be feeling about the questions.

Don't feel you must spend ages talking to the questioner or give a complete explanation of the Goth subculture. The Lady of the

Manners usually answers questions about her darkly whimsical wardrobe with a cheery, "Oh, I always look like this." If pressed for further explanations, a few comments about Tim Burton and Neo-Victorian fashion seem to do the trick. (Or the questioner kindly decides not to pursue any more information and wanders off, shaking his head in amusement.)

There is a particular clueless question the Lady of the Manners has to deal with, and she wonders if other Victorian-esque Goths have been subjected to it too. Starting every year in November, there are sure to be people who look quizzically at the Lady of the Manners and ask, "Oh, are you a Christmas caroler?"

Now, the Lady of the Manners knows that her fondness for wearing top hats is part of what leads to this confused, if well-intentioned, question. Because, to many people, top hats are only worn by Dickens-style Christmas carolers. Combine a top hat with full skirts and a velvet frock coat, and apparently the resemblance to someone who stands on street corners singing "Angels We Have Heard on High" is nigh-on overwhelming. The Lady of the Manners wondered if the sight of her red velvet frock coat was triggering these questions but has since been asked this question while wearing an entirely black outfit, purple lipstick, and a large silver skull brooch pinned to her top hat.

When asked the "Are you a caroler" question, the Lady of the Manners has so far managed to restrain herself from singing something from The Nightmare Before Christmas *and instead just smiles at the questioner and says, "Oh no, I dress like this all the time." But the temptation to burst into song with a gothy Christmas carol is oh so strong . . .*

Mind you, if someone obviously is asking about your appearance just to harass you, feel free to be snarky right back. When the Lady of the Manners encounters people who feel the need to tell her that it isn't Halloween, she usually smiles widely at them, says "Reeeeaaally? Are you sure about that?" and continues on her way. (The people who usually feel the need to make comments like, "Nice costume, Morticia!" tend to be very, er, suburban teens who travel in packs. The last time the Lady of the Manners had an encounter with such a group, she took a step toward the pack of catcalling teen boys while she answered them. Oh, how she *laughed* when the boys, obviously unnerved, all took a step back from her.)

Also, there is no edict handed down from the nonexistent Goth Cabal that says you must scowl at all the people who smile at you. No, really, there isn't. The Lady of the Manners is willing to acknowledge she may be slightly biased about this, as she tends more toward the perky side of Goth, but honestly, Snarklings. This may be a revelation to some of the younger readers, but the sight of you dressed up to the thirteens in your oh-so-dark and spooky finery is absolutely darling. Especially if you are being so very serious about the whole thing. The Lady of the Manners recently saw a pack of babybats loitering about a local shopping area. (Oh, all right, yes. They were mallgoths.) These young babybats had obviously spent a lot of time getting their appearance the way they wanted it, right down to the artfully smudged eye makeup and the tiny stick-on rhinestone cross worn upside down under one eye. The Lady of the Manners was charmed by the babybats and smiled at them as she walked by. Did the babybats smile back? Oh, goodness no, it was glares and scowls all around. For they were spooky and *not* to be smiled at! (Of course, the sullen indignant expressions of the babybats made the Lady of the Manners smile even more widely because she regards very spooky and intense gothlings in much the same way she thinks of puppies or kittens: "Oh, so cute! Look at you. Oh, aren't you fierce! Come here, let me ruffle your hair." The Lady of the Manners tries very hard not to say such things to any babybats or gothlings she meets because she remembers that there is nothing so lowering to a teen as being considered "cute" when he or she is trying to be dark and mysterious. But the Lady of the Manners fears that her facial expressions sometimes betray her "Awwwwww!" thoughts.)

What to do when Goth becomes the darling of the fashion industry

The mainstream fashion industry seems to have a recurring fondness for borrowing from the Goth subculture. Every couple of years, the stores are full of velvet jackets, flowing skirts, and lace blouses. So what should any self-respecting Goth do in the face of this? Wait for the clearance sales, of course!

Oh, all right, that was a bit on the short and flippant side, wasn't it? But that doesn't mean it's a wrong answer. The Lady of the Manners has seen this sort of thing happen before, and mainstream fashion's fascination with black lace and velvet usually lasts for about three months. If you can hang on that long, the clearance racks, thrift stores, and re-sale boutiques will be filled with all sorts of lovely things.

Of course, that's only one part of the dilemma. Whenever the gothic style becomes more popular, complete strangers will increasingly stop you in the street to ask questions, usually about what you're wearing and where they can find something just like it.

No, you may not snarl or snap at the well-meaning trendy people. Not even if you're having a particularly bad day. However, your answers don't have to be overwhelmingly helpful either. The Lady of the Manners has answered recent "Where did you get it?!" questions with "I found it at a thrift store" or "Oh, I don't remember. I've had it for years and years," which leaves the trendy people blinking confusedly.

Now, the Lady of the Manners can see some of you getting very fierce and uncomfortable with the idea that people can scamper down to the mall and, with a bit of determined spending, disguise themselves as a Real Goth. "Tourists!" The Lady of the Manners can hear you cry derisively. "They're just doing it because it's trendy!" There, there, it's all right. Have you gotten that out of your system? Now, pay attention. Yes, it's true, there will be more people disguised as one of us for a little bit. However, just because someone is wearing head-to-toe Gothic Victorian ruffles doesn't mean her disguise is perfect. People dressing that way because it's the latest trend never seem quite comfortable with it; they have that faint but unmistakable air of someone wearing a costume, someone who is following what the media tells her to do instead of dressing that way because that's who she is. It's a subtle but unmistakable distinction.

Every time popular culture or fashion borrows from the darker side of the subcultural map, some people get very cross and territorial about *their* look and *their* scene. The Lady of the Manners finds such fervor endearing but on the whole not terribly helpful. You see, each and every person involved in the Goth scene had to start somewhere, and some of those people discovered their bat wings later than others. Yes, roll your eyes at people wearing "Gothic Fashion Savvy" T-shirts, but don't automatically dismiss everyone who dabbles in darker fashions.

As an example, the Lady of the Manners merely has to point to the proliferation of skull-festooned clothing, jewelry, and home decor items that have become readily available. How much power can a symbol retain if it is so (if you'll pardon the phrase) defanged that it is turning up in teen accessory stores across the land?

The Lady of the Manners does *not* believe that a person must provide proof of his or her subcultural "cred" before being allowed to own skull-festooned goodies. Not at all. But the Lady of the Manners does admit to occasionally having to quash an impulse to ask complete strangers what drew them to the skull necklace, shirt, or rain boots they're wearing. Was it because they are interested in the symbolic meaning of the skull (or skull and crossbones)? Was it because they thought it was "edgy" and "fashion forward" (buzzwords the Lady of the Manners despises)? Or was it simply that they are big fans of the *Pirates of the Caribbean* movies? The Lady of the Manners would like to think that the ever-growing crop of cute skull merchandise is a sign that mainstream society is finally accepting the Goth and other alternative subcultures. (Trust the Lady of the Manners on this, Snarklings. The way mainstream society shows its acceptance is through readily available consumer goods targeted at one's particular subculture.)

While the Lady of the Manners is completely in favor of taking advantage of the fashion industry's seasonal dabblings in darkness, the Lady of the Manners is also all in favor of being an informed consumer. Do some research, read reviews, and take a close look at items before purchasing them. Just because something is made by a name brand doesn't automatically make it any better than the old standbys; in fact, sometimes it means the quality is worse because those name brands are trying to cash in on what they think is a short-lived trend.

The basics of assembling a gothy wardrobe

Where to buy Gothic clothes? Why, everywhere! Everywhere, that is, if you're willing to put a smidge of effort into assembling your wardrobe and are not just looking to buy pre-packaged *gawthick* items. Just about every place that sells clothing offers items in black; as tempting as it is to amass a collection of highly ornate, one-of-a-kind items, even the Lady of the Manners has to admit it is more . . . practical to have a selection of basics to build upon. (Forgive the Lady of the Manners, Snarklings. She needs a moment to get over the shock of advocating anything practical with regard to clothing.)

But that means all you need to do to dress gothy is to buy a bunch of black clothes, right? Well, it's not quite *that* easy. If it were, a bunch of corporate "suit" types would be very surprised to find out they have a new subcultural affiliation.

So what are the basic building blocks of the Goth closet? The following list is designed to help you build an "everyday" Goth wardrobe, not a club-going wardrobe. Yes, many of the items can do double-duty as day wear *and* club wear, but the main point of this list is to recommend a good collection of pieces you can mix and match for daily wear. The Lady of the Manners would like to point out that you should be able to assemble at least one outfit appropriate for job interviews from these basics.

- First and foremost, get yourself a lint roller. Just trust the Lady of the Manners on this one, okay? If you're going to indulge in a wardrobe of gloom, you absolutely need a lint roller. Or two or seven or thirteen, stashed at home, in the car, and in your office.

- Some well-fitting, well-pressed dress shirts in black, white, and a dark jewel tone such as red, deep blue, or violet. (This goes for both ladies and gentlemen, by the way.) Feel free to branch out and search for variations in the cut of the sleeves (French cuffs, buttons, frilly), collar (high, ruffled, extremely pointy), or even pattern (the Lady of the Manners has a fondness for stripes, while other Goths collect shirts in baroque wallpaper prints).

- Two different black blazers. Yes, *two*. One in black velvet and one in some other less dressy fabric. Mind you, if you follow in the pointy-toed footsteps of the Lady of the Manners, you will end up accumulating many, many black blazers, all in slightly different fabrics and cuts, and perhaps some with skull or heart patches. But you don't *really* need a bazillion faintly identical black blazers; two will be enough to allow you to put together all sorts of charming ensembles.

- At least two pairs of well-fitting black trousers. (That is, if you are the trouser-wearing type. The Lady of the Manners is not a member of the trouser-wearing collective.) Black trousers are a basic staple of all sorts of different wardrobe styles, and Goth is no exception to that.

- For the ladies, at least three skirts of different fabrics or length. Skirts that look good layered on top of each other are ideal. The Lady of the Manners strongly suggests that at least one them be an ankle-length, full-circle type of skirt, because that sort of skirt can be used as a petticoat under other long skirts or pinned up to form a bustle-type overskirt.

 Again for the ladies, a well-fitting black dress. It doesn't have to be a fancy party dress, but a black dress that makes you look put together with minimum effort is worth *more* than its weight in gold.

 Stripy socks or tights. Yes, many people consider these to be for Halloween and mallgoths only, but the Lady of the Manners would beg to differ. The flash of a striped leg from beneath a black skirt or trouser can be a subtle nod to the style your heart holds dear. Not to mention the Lady of the Manners has seen more and more "high-end" fashion labels selling striped tights and stockings at a shocking mark-up. (A word to the wise: the striped tights that spring up on the shelves at drug stores every-where during October? Those are perfectly good quality stripy tights. In fact, they're the same quality as the tights stocked year-round at various "alternative" stores. The Lady of the Manners herself just stocks up on stripy tights in October and uses them throughout the year. Why pay twelve dollars or more for stripy tights when you can pur-chase the exact same ones for three dollars in October?) If stripes really aren't your thing, look for narrow-weave black fishnets, vintage-style black lace, polka dots, or any of the other interesting patterns that turn up in the ho-siery department.

 One pair each of black shoes and boots, both of which ab-solutely need to be in good condition and should be sturdy enough that you can walk (or run) to catch public transit while wearing them.

 A basic black coat of some sort. (The Lady of the Manners covers this in the section on dressing for winter weather.)

Another good thing about a collection of basics is that they are easy to customize. For example, you can change the buttons on the blazer or shirt. If you're feeling really crafty, buy a kit for making your own fabric-covered buttons. (The Lady of the Manners has a stockpile of buttons covered in pink taffeta to add to whatever strikes her fancy and is still searching for fabric with a good skull print in order to start making her own skull buttons.) Add band patches and pins (you can make your own designs for patches by using iron on transfer paper with an ink-jet printer, or you can paint or stencil designs onto fabric, cut them out, and use them for patches). Make your own appliqués by tracing a design onto fusible interfacing (found at any fabric store), ironing the interfacing onto fabric, cutting out the design, and then sewing on the appliqué. Try your hand at embroidered details, be they a decorative stitch in a contrasting thread or black-on-black designs to add a subtle flair. Find someplace that sells safety pins in bulk quantities and cover side seams in them. (If you want to go really over-the-top, take apart the garment along the seams and then "sew" it back together using rows and rows of safety pins.) If you're skillful at drawing, use fabric paint or bleach pens to add designs to any garment you wish. Grommet tape (wide cotton ribbon with grommets placed every inch or so) is now readily available at most fabric and craft stores; sew that down two of the back seams of a jacket or dress and use ribbon to create corset-style lacing.

The Lady of the Manners's favorite stores are thrift shops, consignment boutiques, eBay, and Etsy.com. In fact, when the Lady of the Manners isn't writing, she is sure to be found altering and decorating her latest clothing find. Yes, searching through thrift stores and customizing items does take time and patience, but it is worth the effort if you want to avoid looking like a run-of-the-mill mallgoth. There is immense satisfaction in being able to answer, "Oh, I made it!" when someone asks you where you got a particular item of clothing.

Speaking of "Oh, I made it!"—learn to sew. Wait, don't run

away in terror. While learning how to sew things completely from scratch is the ideal path, learning how to sew just enough so you can do your own alterations is *essential*. It doesn't take professional-level sewing skills to sew on buttons or add some trim; it just takes patience. Teach yourself tailoring skills on inexpensive clothes you buy at thrift stores; while the Lady of the Manners still regards making a dress from scratch with a bit of apprehension, she feels no such qualms about unpicking the hem and lining from a jacket so she can add darts to enhance its hourglass silhouette. You can add rows and rows of decorative trim, ribbon, lace, fringe, feathers, or just about any other sort of embellishment to clothing, and it all can be done by hand with a needle and thread. Yes, a sewing machine will allow you to go faster, but sitting on the couch and sewing trim on to an item of clothing while a silly vampire movie plays in the background is a time-honored Goth activity.

If you're absolutely fumble-fingered and have an irrational terror of sewing machines, then start saving your pennies and have things custom made for you. (An aside: Please do not be one of those people who complains about how expensive custom clothing is. Custom clothing is made by small businesses run by artisans, and they can't use cost-cutting tricks, such as mass production in faraway countries, that larger clothing companies can. Those artisans deserve every penny they earn, so please don't try to haggle with them or whine about the cost. The polite thing to do is thank them for their time, effort, and creativity, which are all devoted to making you look beautiful.)

Learn to develop an eye for quality construction and materials. There is no point in spending money on a shoddily constructed garment that will fade or snag after a few washing. No, not even if the garment is adorned with skulls or other enticing gothy iconography. Again, this is where thrift stores are far, far better for Goths than regular retail establishments. Yes, it takes time and patience to put together a wardrobe full of shadowy loveliness from thrift stores, but it's time well spent.

Another aside: The Lady of the Manners feels she must mention a certain item of "Goth" clothing that carries some rather unfortunate connotations. You know those baggy pants that are liberally festooned with chains and straps? The Lady of the Manners isn't really sure where why those sorts of trousers became the fashion but suspects it stems from a strange intermingling of more industrial fashions with . . . something else. However, where they came from isn't the important thing. No, the thing to know about these pants is that they are an almost sure sign that the wearer is a mallgoth, a spooky teen trying to look more, er, menacing than he ever could be. No, Snarklings, this isn't just one of the Lady of the Manners's unreasonable biases; to most Goths, huge baggy pants with extraneous hardware give off a faint but unmistakable air of ridiculousness. The Lady of the Manners (and other Goths, of course) are all in favor of over-the-top apparel and accessories, but something about the oversized, jingling pants seems to miss over-the-top and go straight to, well, silly. If you are a devotee of these trousers, don't feel you must give them up. Just be aware that other Goths may look at you and roll their eyes a teensy bit, especially if you happen to be in your teenage years.

Another thing you must remember, if you become a devotee of more elaborate styles, is that you must pay attention to the details. It is not enough to throw on a frilly dress or shirt and blazer; make sure you've put the same thought into the rest of your look.

Do your socks (or stockings or tights) and footwear go with the rest of your outfit? Or, if not, do they communicate that you are deliberately going for a mixed-up look? The same ideas apply to hair, makeup, hats, gloves, jewelry, and any other bits and bobs. Paying attention to the details will help ensure that you don't look like you're wearing a Goth-themed costume.

While you're paying attention to those details, the Lady of the Manners will let you in on one of the most exasperating challenges for Goths. Make sure your blacks match! Oh, yes, Snarklings, there are different shades of black. It may seem silly, but this can be very noticeable, especially with cotton, rayon, or other natural fibers. Black fabric can have green, brownish, red, or blue undertones, and these differences are emphasized when two different fabrics are worn together. While you can get away with wearing brown-black and red-black garments together, or green-black and blue-black, if you put a red-black item next to a green-black one, you're suddenly looking at Christmastime in a black hole. It's quite vexing.

What can you do when faced with such a problem? First, look at yourself in a mirror under bright light, and then think about what light you'll be in when wearing the outfit. If you're going out to a darkened club, don't worry about it too much; club lighting hides all sorts of things, including slightly mismatched blacks. The Lady of the Manners knows of other Goths who run everything through a black dye bath, but she herself has gotten mixed results from such projects. If you're one of those amazingly organized types, you could group your garments by their various undertones so that you won't suffer any green vs. red issues. Or you could decide to try your best but know that if your blacks clash, it isn't the end of the world. Goodness knows that sometimes the Lady of the Manners has to embrace this point of view; otherwise, she would never leave the house.

Why no one really has an "original" Goth look, so get over yourselves already

The Lady of the Manners has heard all sorts of grumbles like, "So and so stole my style!" or "So and so accused me of ripping off her look!" Which, after much thought, has led the Lady of the Manners to this conclusion:

No one in this scene has an original look, Snarklings. Get over yourselves.

Hmmm. That came out a bit snippier than the Lady of the Manners intended; forgive her. But nonetheless, the sentiment holds true. Everyone has influenced everyone else at this point. Even the "original Goth look" was lifted from early horror films, Victorian mourning clothes, punk, and new wave/new romantic. Way back when, one of the founding principals of this subculture was a certain style. You remember—black clothes (mostly velvet, lace, and fishnet), ruffles, pale face makeup, lots of eyeliner, black lipstick? Any of this ring a bell? Anyway, it used to be that if you saw someone dressed in that manner, you could probably assume he or she was a Goth. This also meant most gothy clothing tended to be a bit similar. Nowadays, you'd be hard-pressed to identify other Goths on the street solely by their clothes. Yes, some people still adhere to the "I'm a vampire from a Hammer horror film" look, but there are just as many cybergoths in reflective clothing or Jeans 'n' T-shirt Goths who blow the subculture fashion template to smithereens. Not to mention all the other style tribes that share stylistic borders with Gothland! No, you no longer can just look at someone with pink and black hair and skull accessories and assume she's a Goth. She might be emo, a scenekid, a metalhead, or another fellow subcultural traveler, or she might just be someone who just does a lot of shopping at Claire's Accessories and Hot Topic.

Which is why the Lady of the Manners is so amused by this uproar. When the Lady of the Manners sees another young lady dressed in formal Victorian-esque funeral garb, the Lady of the Manners does not start grumbling that this new girl "stole her look" but instead goes over and strikes up a conversation with her. The other girl might share other interests with the Lady of the Manners, leading to more conversations and a new friendship. Or she might know of some exciting new stores or designers for the Lady of the Manners to investigate. The Lady of the Manners is also heartened to see that someone else will be on the dance floor wearing a bustle and a big hat—it makes people more careful with lit cigarettes, for one thing.

The funniest part of this whole thing (in the Lady of the Manners's opinion) is the fact that she's been hearing these comments from people who are wearing . . . oh, goodness, there's no delicate way to put this . . . off-the-rack gothwear. If you are wearing an item of clothing from a nationally distributed clothing label, you don't get to complain about others dressing like you. (Yes, that means you Miss/Mister "My whole wardrobe is by Lip Service/Tripp/Shrine." While the clothes can be very nice, they are *not* original, one-of-a-kind fashions.)

Does this mean the Lady of the Manners snubs other gothy sorts who do wear clothes from those labels, and that you should too? Goodness, no. The Lady of the Manners quite likes and purchases some of the mass-produced gothwear available. She thinks the fact that someone's making a profit by selling clothing for freaks and eccentrics shows how far the Goth subculture has come. However, this *does* mean the Lady of the Manners will gently laugh at someone wearing an ensemble bought at Hot Topic who complains that others are stealing his style. If you can buy it in a national chain store, you aren't allowed to consider it your very own idea.

Many ElderGoths have been known to cast aspersions on the mere existence of Hot Topic, but the Lady of the Manners doesn't really understand why. Yes, if anyplace would sell an "insta-Goth" kit, Hot Topic would, but that doesn't make it bad. It isn't even a bad thing that people who are just . . . flirting with the whole Goth thing can pop 'round to HT and buy a whole spooooooky wardrobe and unnatural hair dye with their parents' credit card. (Stop gritting your teeth. It *isn't* a bad thing.) When the Lady of the Manners was a suburban-dwelling teenager, she would have given anything to have had a Hot Topic in a mall near her. What you all have to remember is that because Hot Topic is a national chain, the Goth subculture is now more visible to the mainstream. This means more people are aware of it, which means that if everyone associated with the subculture takes up the Lady of the Manners's cause of politeness, maybe (just maybe) Goths will quit getting labeled as "baby-eating Satanic murderers" and merely be labeled as "those people who wear black and dye their hair funny colors." Mass awareness can lead to more understanding and less stereotyping—we just have to work at it.

But to return to the notion that no Goth is quite the singularly unique dark snowflake he or she would like to think, the Lady of the Manners would like to add is that it *is* in terribly poor taste to copy someone exactly. Look at the pretty people around you and get ideas, by all means. Take a look at Goth-flavored photo shoots and websites. Just don't try to look like someone's identical twin. The idea is that you find your own interpretation of the Goth style—not that you say, "I want to look just like so-and-so" and mimic his or her every accessory. While it's perfectly all right to be inspired by someone else's look, people find it uncomfortable to be confronted by their clone. Not to mention that if you decide to imitate someone's look down to the skull earrings and tiny top hat, you have crossed over that invisible border to costume town. People may assume that you assembled your outfit in an homage and make comments that reflect that line of thought. ("Nice costume! Does so-and-so know you dressed like him tonight?") You have been warned, and don't say the Lady of the Manners didn't tell you so.

For many Goths, part of the allure of our darkly glamorous subculture is that (to borrow a line from a song by Ministry that always fills the Goth dance floor) everyday *is* Halloween. We Goths have stepped out of the binding confines of mainstream fashion into a comfortably shadowy realm that allows us to express ourselves in a more elaborate fashion. The Lady of the Manners fervently hopes that all of you realize expressing yourself should be fun. Don't worry that other people might give you strange looks or make comments. So what? In spite of what countless teens have believed through the years, people don't expire after someone looks at them oddly. Instead of worrying about what strangers might be thinking, the Lady of the Manners encourages you to use that energy to transform yourself into who you want to be, inside *and* out.

NINE

Dance the Ghost with Me: Music and Gothy Club and Concert Etiquette

The never-ending debate about music vs. fashion (part 2)

"Goth is *really* about music. Anyone can slap on some eyeliner and throw on some black clothes, but if you're a Real Goth, you know it's really about the music." This statement represents the other side of the great Goth argument that is always going on somewhere. As the Lady of the Manners pointed out in the previous chapter about fashion, it's an argument that, in addition to being never-ending, gets very heated.

"Waitaminute!" The Lady of the Manners just knows you're saying. "You talked about this in the previous chapter, and you were all, "Well, duh, it's about fashion!" Are you changing your mind?" No, not quite. While it's true that the Lady of the Manners is a devotee of dark frills and jet-beaded mourning attire, she very much believes you cannot separate the music from the fashion. No, you can't, not really, so stop giving her that funny look.

Goth crept out from the long shadow thrown by the punk movement. If it hadn't been for bands such as Joy Division, Siouxsie and the Banshees, Bauhaus, and The Cure, Goth would not be what it is today. Would the Goth subculture still be around? Oh, the Lady of the Manners is certain of it. But it wouldn't be the same pale creature swaying in a darkened nightclub to sonorous rhythms punctuating a melody in a minor key.

"So what is Goth music, then?" Oh . . . dear. The Lady of the Manners has been asked this question time and time again and still doesn't really have a comprehensive answer to it. There are bands (such as the four named in the previous paragraph) that are widely acknowledged as being the progenitors of the Gothic musical genre (even if all of them have denied it, at one point or another). But not all Goth music sounds even remotely like those bands. Some sounds like morbid carnival and cabaret music and other music straddles the sometimes very fuzzy border between Goth and metal. There are splinter genres for every potential offshoot of Goth music you could possibly imagine: gothabilly, dark folk, se-

piachord, ethereal, synthpop and ebm, deathrock, post-punk, dark orchestral music, goth-industrial . . . the list goes on and on. That isn't even taking into consideration the wide range of performers usually popular with Goths who wouldn't really fall under the black parasol of the Goth label. (Tom Waits, anyone?) Even those bands considered to be the roots from which the Goth movement sprang aren't always universally adored by all Goths. (The Lady of the Manners thinks fondly of Joy Division as charming-if-moody ancestors of Goth but really would rather listen to something else, if you don't mind.)

In the Lady of the Manners's experience, just about any band that could be labeled Goth will at some point be the topic of a "Are you kidding? They're not Goth, they're ———!" debate. No matter if a band sets out to be the spookiest collection of musicians this side of the grave, somewhere some other Goth will be busily posting on the Internet about how that band isn't *really* Goth, and if people wanted to hear Real Goth music, they should listen to ——— band instead. Which is all good fun, if you can distance yourself from the inevitable flame wars and name-calling that always surround such posts. Personally, the Lady of the Manners feels that people should listen to whatever music happens to catch their fancy. Yes, if you've decided to be part of the Goth subculture, you should know your musical history and be aware of what bands you are likely to hear at a Goth club, but don't feel you can't listen to a band that doesn't have a bat-shaped stamp of approval from that nonexistent Goth Cabal. Also, don't feel ashamed of whatever music you might have listened to before you wandered over to the dark side. It doesn't matter if you listened to country, classical, disco, or the most sugar-coated boybands ever to saturate the airwaves. Very few Goths went through childhood with a soundtrack of dark and atmospheric music.

The Lady of the Manners has a pet theory that most Goth ladies of a certain age (meaning mid-thirties and up) came to the subculture via three separate paths: the punk path (after all, deathrock started out as an offshoot of punk and post-punk but added a dash of Ziggy Stardust glam rock, whiteface makeup, extra zombies, and cheesy B-horror movies); the metal path (power chords and boys in eyeliner made for an easy transition to more power chords and boys in eyeliner, with an extra emphasis on vampires); and the swirly dark romantic pop path (otherwise known as the "I want to dress just like Stevie Nicks!" route to Gothdom). Scoff all you want, but every other Goth lady of a certain age the Lady of the Manners has explained this theory to has nodded her head in agreement. (The Lady of the Manners is sorry to admit that she has no accompanying theory for Goth gentlemen of a certain age, but she assumes the theory holds equally true in regard to the gentlemen, give or take some details.)

While the Lady of the Manners knows some babybats who are, in effect, second-generation Goths who *have* been raised on a steady musical diet of The Cure and Danny Elfman, most Goths have at least a few Top 40 musical skeletons hiding in their darkened closets.

For that matter, don't feel that you must only listen to Goth-approved music and nothing else. It would be silly for a subculture based on finding beauty and interest in different and sometimes dark places to be deliberately closed-minded about music. And while the Lady of the Manners herself has been the target of gentle teasing about some of the bands she listens to, she refuses to let anyone tell her that she *can't* enjoy them. (The Lady of the Manners would like to take this opportunity to mention, as a tangent about music *and* fashion, that attending something like a My Chemical Romance or Rob Zombie concert while dressed in full Victorian Gothic regalia provides vast entertainment.) Besides, DJs at Goth clubs seem fond of experimenting with which "mainstream" pop hit will still pack the dance floor. The Lady of the Manners has heard reports from trustworthy friends about every black-clad creature of the night charging to the dance floor with glee when the opening strains of "Baby Got Back" or "Beat It" come throbbing out of the speakers.

Why the ElderGoths are always so cranky about the mainstream eyeliner-wearing band du jour

Every few years or so, it seems, a musical act emerges, and the mainstream media tags it with the Goth moniker. Maybe it's because they sing about scary or depressing subjects, maybe it's because their music videos have a dark and spooky tone, or maybe it's because they're photographed wearing black clothes and heavy eyeliner. And when the mainstream media starts throwing the Goth label around, you can be sure that the older members of the Goth community will be rolling their eyes and denouncing the newly labeled musical act. (Sometimes without even listening to anything by the band. That's how ingrained this response is.)

But why? Isn't it possible that this new band is indeed Goth? Or at least related to Goth and should be given a chance? Well, yes. But ElderGoths are set in their ways and have something of a knee-jerk reaction to anything from the mainstream barging in to our precious and dark little corner of the world. We are too unique, too special, too (to again quote Lydia from *Beetlejuice*) "strange and unusual" to have anything to do with mainstream culture.

But! That sort of stance (which is indeed prevalent amongst a lot of ElderGoths) oh-so-conveniently ignores the fact that many bands beloved by Goths were *also* beloved by the mainstream. The Cure, Siouxsie and the Banshees, Bauhaus, The Sisters of Mercy, Love and Rockets, Peter Murphy, The Smiths—all of these artists had songs that did well in the charts. (The pop music history of the U.K. includes even more bands of Goth interest that cracked the charts.) Does this mean those ElderGoths are being elitist hypocrites? Er, not quite. As the Lady of the Manners sees it, the knee-jerk ElderGoth dismissal of new, possibly Goth-ish but certainly mainstream bands is laced with an unhealthy dose of defensiveness about the "age-appropriateness" of Goth. The average person associates Goth with teenagers and their fads and phases. (If the Lady of the Manners never again hears the statement, "Oh, I used to be a Goth, but I *grew out of it*," it still will be too soon.) In the Lady of the Manners's experience, most mainstream-ish bands being labeled as Goth tend to have a rather large fan base amongst the, well, younger crowd. When that fact is combined with the ridiculous notion that Goth is a teen trend marketed by Hot Topic, is it any wonder the ElderGoth crowd is quick to roll its eyes and deride any new band labeled "Goth"?

Speaking of Hot Topic and other chain-store marketing, another reason that ElderGoths are usually so cranky about that Goth label is that while the musicians may be well aware of the musical history their sound references (or pays homage to), the younger fans of the band frequently have little to no idea about the musical roots. They just see their idols wearing some sort of cool shirt, and hey, they can buy one just like it at the mall! (One of the Lady of the Manners's friends has frequently stated that she wants to go up to any of the babybats or other alterna-teens wearing Misfits shirts and demand that they name at least five songs by the band.) Or the younger fans hear a really cool song and have no idea it is a cover of a previous musician's work. When an ElderGoth mentions the original musician, the younger gothlings stare with no recognition in their eyes; worse, the Lady of the Manners has heard of the younger gothling vigorously arguing that the cover is actually the original version of the song and that any other version must be a rip-off. None of this is going to make the ElderGoths feel kindly toward newer, possibly more mainstream musical acts.

While the Lady of the Manners understands and sympathizes with all the reasons behind her fellow ElderGoths' derision toward whatever eyeliner be-smeared band is currently on heavy rotation on MTV, she at times wishes they weren't quite so vehement and venomous in their dismissal. No, the majority of those bands aren't Goth. But they have Goth influences, and maybe, just maybe, might be worth investigating.

Why Marilyn Manson is not a Goth

Let's get one thing clear, right at the start: Marilyn Manson's music is not Goth. It is more properly categorized as metal. Fun concerts full of over-the-top spectacle, but not Goth. Yes, the Lady of the Manners just knows some people from the metal subculture are, at this very instant, growling with rage at the notion of Marilyn Manson's music being called "metal." The Lady of the Manners is well aware that there are as many different subgenres of metal as there are of Goth, and that droves and droves of metal fans can't agree as to whether or not they should consider Mr. Manson's musical efforts part of their subculture. But from an outside-the-faithful point of view, Marilyn Manson's shock-rock musical theatrics with loud guitars fit the metal label quite tidily. He's a direct musical descendant of Alice Cooper and Kiss, with a few dashes of David Bowie and Ozzy Osbourne thrown in for good measure.

Now, what about Mr. Manson himself? Even though many people dismiss Mr. Manson as being no longer relevant to anything going on in music or pop culture, he is, for whatever reason, still referred to as a Goth by members of the mainstream media and people outside the subculture. So is he a Goth? Well, the Lady of the Manners doesn't have a definitive answer to that, nor should she claim to. No one can really answer that question other than Mr. Manson himself. However, based on interviews with Mr. Manson that the Lady of the Manners has read, the evidence does seem to be mounting. He has a striking, decadent, and dark personal style. He's espoused an interest in decaying and (again) decadent ideas and themes and prefers to present a highly stylized image whenever he is in the public eye. And, according to interviews with his friends and romantic partners, he is a perfect gentleman; courteous, considerate, and well-mannered. All of which, in the Lady of the Manners's book, means that, yes, Wednesday and Pugsley, Marilyn Manson *is* a Goth.

(The Lady of the Manners is sure that Mr. Manson has been waiting with bated breath for the Lady of the Manners's validation of his gothness. Sure of it, she tells you, and don't you try to convince her differently.)

Now, do the above-mentioned reasons explain why the mainstream media and others always mention Marilyn Manson in connection with Goth? To a degree (that striking and dark personal style certainly helps), but the Lady of the Manners suspects the real reason is that Mr. Manson unnerves a lot of people. He's perceived as extremely dark, very spooky (weren't his legions of young fans referred to as "spooky kids"? They certainly were where the Lady of the Manners lives), and, to many people, unsettlingly creepy. And like it or not, to the average person out there, those same traits apply to the Goth subculture. Which means that whenever the shadow of Goth surfaces in the mainstream (especially in the U.S.), someone is sure to dig up a picture of Marilyn Manson in order to make a point. So what should the rest of us in the Goth subculture do when that happens? Well, not throw a complete hissy fit about Marilyn Manson not being a Real Goth, for one thing. Starting flame wars and arguments about it won't help matters and will only reinforce the idea that Goths are immature and argumentative. If someone asks you directly, then of course you should share your views on the matter. But don't get defensive every time the media equates Marilyn Manson (or other dark shock-rock bands, for that matter) with Goth. Instead, try changing people's minds by being an example of what you think a Goth should be.

Manners on the dance floor

Goths and dancing are closely intertwined. The most common social activity for Goths is going out to the local Goth club (with the social activity of *getting ready* to go out to the local Goth club coming in at a close second). Gathering together in gloom-shrouded clubs dressed in dark finery and swirling around a dance floor to a morbid tune is the skeleton that the Goth subculture is built upon. Younger *gothlings* and *babybats* long for the night they'll be old enough to mingle with the dark and glamorous throng, while *ElderGoths* speak wistfully of times past when they were able to survive on four hours of sleep a night and still function at work the next day.

Yes, more and more cities are enacting laws to prohibit smoking in clubs, bars, and restaurants. Many of the Lady of the Manners's friends get quite up in arms about these laws, complaining (understandably) that such laws are nasty pieces of interfering nonsense, enacted and supported by people who want to police what other people do. The Lady of the Manners does understand those objections—really she does! But as a nonsmoker, the Lady of the Manners is rather grateful that she can go out for a night at the local Goth club and not come home reeking of stale cigarette smoke, even if she knows how to remove such odors from her black-frilled finery.

You would think that since going out dancing is such an important social activity for Goths, everyone in our gloomy little subculture would instinctively know how to behave when out swooping and stomping on the dance floor. Sadly, you would be wrong. Very wrong. So what are some common faux pas and mishaps Goths have to deal with while swaying and swirling to "Bela Lugosi's Dead"?

Oh, how about cigarettes and drinks? If the Lady of the Manners had her way, no one would ever take a lit cigarette onto a dance floor ever again. Because it seems that the people who feel the need to smoke while dancing

aren't content with just keeping the cigarette in their mouths— oh no. They invariably feel the need to transcribe mysterious lines and arcs in the air with it and usually don't pay any attention to the fact that *there are other people around them*. Burning someone's flesh or damaging her clothing is, as a matter of fact, terribly rude. If you discover you are responsible for such a thing, apologize immediately to the person you singed, and ask if the damage to her wardrobe is minor. Offers of first aid and repairs or replacements to clothing would also not be amiss. Now, the Lady of the Manners has heard indignant responses from smokers about this, such as "People shouldn't be wearing stuff to the club they're worried about getting damaged anyway!" Sorry, oh smoke-wreathed Snarklings, but the Lady of the Manners does not agree. If you aren't able to keep from singeing or damaging someone with your lit cigarette, you are the one at fault.

Much the same thing applies to taking drinks out onto the dance floor. The Lady of the Manners used to be adamantly against drinks on the dance floor, but now she believes that the potential for spills, alcohol-soaked clothing, and accidents from wet floors do not counterbalance the grim possibility of someone's drink being dosed when he or she isn't there to keep a close eye on it. What this means, however, is that if you have a beverage and hear a song you must go dance to, you should ask a friend to keep an eye on your drink. If there isn't anyone nearby who you trust to guard your drink, or if the song being played is so compelling that all of you are rushing the floor, by all means, take your drink with you. Just be *very* careful with it while dancing; no extravagant arm gestures, no pogoing, etc. If you do spill your beverage, let one of the club staff know so it can be cleaned up. (That is, if the clubs you go to care about drinks spilled on the floor. The Goth clubs that the Lady of the Manners attends do, but she realizes that some clubs may have a more punk rock, devil-may-care approach to such things.) If, heaven forfend, you end up drenching someone with the contents of your glass, promptly apologize and ask if there's anything you can do to help clean up the mess. That includes offering to pay any dry cleaning costs.

Speaking of extravagant arm gestures and such, Goth dancing tends toward the more interpretive style, what with the dramatic flinging of hands, swooping around, and other such theatrics. (The Lady of the Manners says this with all possible fondness and with perhaps a smidge of self-mockery. Just a smidge.) This means that all the dancers must be aware of their surroundings, not just the ones with lit cigarettes or full drinks. It's rude to smack a fellow dance floor denizen with an outflung hand, no matter how "signature" a move it is for you. Not to mention that with the elaborate outfits, jewelry, and hairstyles favored by Goths, a dramatic swooping movement could cause you to become very awkwardly tangled up with another person. (The Lady of the Manners has many such memories of herself and friends having to slink off the dance floor to disentangle assorted fluttering veils, lace trains, and rosaries that had accidentally tied them together. Untangling ourselves was the easy part; managing to exit the dance floor to the beat like we had *intended* to entangle ourselves was another trick entirely.)

If you are one of the Goths who, like the Lady of the Manners, favors elaborate outfits with trailing sleeves, flaring coat skirts, hats, bustles, yards and yards of petticoats, or other assorted fripperies, please be sure you know how to manage and contain your sartorial extravagance. It takes a certain amount of skill and grace to swirl about a crowded dance floor and not knock anyone over with your petticoats and bustle, and there is nothing wrong with practicing such things in the privacy of your own home, particularly when your blinds are closed, before becoming a dance floor tragedy.

Manners and socializing at the club (including "don't touch people without invitation" and "always be nice to the staff")

Of course, you have to be aware of more than just dance floor etiquette when you go to a Goth club. The Lady of the Manners has previously mentioned some of these: the club is not a petting zoo, and you shouldn't touch anyone without asking *and* being told that it's okay. (Yes, that includes touching someone's clothing and hair or offering friendly back rubs. The Lady of the Manners knows that many Goths consider their local club to be a safe space, and having people you barely know or don't consider close friends come up and touch you, no matter how friendly they think they're being, is disconcerting to say the least.)

Another thing the Lady of the Manners mentioned in other chapters is to *always* be polite to the staff at the club. If an employee asks you to move or stop behaving in a certain way, do not argue. On the other hand, don't take it upon yourself to act like a club employee when you are not; as a patron of a club, you have the right to complain about people's behavior but not the authority to make them leave. Along these lines, don't expect to be on the guest list for an event unless someone associated with the club has specifically told you so, and don't pull the "But don't you know who I am?!" routine to get away with not paying for drinks or a cover charge. Speaking of paying for drinks, tip the bar staff. If you cannot afford to tip the staff, you shouldn't be buying drinks. That may seem a tad harsh, but it's true. Also do not assume the bar staff are there for your amusement; they are a captive audience and have to put up with a lot of attention they may not want, including flirtation and inappropriate comments, so don't make their job any more difficult than it already is.

Why does the Lady of the Manners keep going on and on about club etiquette? Because going to the local Goth club is one of the major social activities in the Goth subculture, and nothing can turn a night sour and annoying faster than having to deal with rude people at "your" club. And yes, the rude people sometimes are other Goths. Some of the Lady of the Manners's friends who work at nightclubs have told her absolute horror stories about other club-going Goths who apparently think their all-black wardrobe gives them an automatic pass to behave like boors and treat the staff like wayward servants. Which, of course, is nonsense. Being someplace with loud music, dim lighting, and alcohol does not mean you should abandon civilized behavior.

Being polite to the staff at the club includes the DJs. When requesting a song, try to know the title and artist. Don't go up expecting the DJ to read your mind or be able to identify a song just because you can hum the chorus. If the DJ tells you that a song by that artist already has been played, don't throw a tantrum or insist on getting your way. And if the DJ does play your request, go dance to it, for goodness' sake! (The Lady of the Manners's DJ friends have ranted quite a bit about people who request songs but can't be bothered to dance to them.)

Of course, DJs need to practice basic courtesy too. Don't roll your eyes or sneer when someone comes up to request an "old favorite." Just because you're tired of certain songs does not mean that the club patrons are. While the Lady of the Manners understands that DJs want to play new music they're excited about, they need to remember that for many, part of the attraction of going to a Goth club is the chance to get dressed up and dance to the music that makes them happy. Yes, even if that music is almost thirty years old and has been played in Goth clubs since the scene started. There are Goth clubs and DJs who enforce a certain thing known as a *do not request* list. It's exactly what it sounds like, a list of songs that the DJ refuses to play. The Lady of the Manners

thinks that such lists are a touch rude, really. The Lady of the Manners understands that DJs and club employees can get tired of certain songs very quickly, but that is no reason to completely ban a song from ever being heard in a club. You certainly don't have to play "This Corrosion" or "Dead Stars" every Friday night, but you shouldn't refuse to play a song *ever again*.

(Contrariwise, the Lady of the Manners has known of DJs who played the same thing from week to week, to the point where the club patrons could predict the order of almost every song, and that sort of thing got a bit, well, tiring. By all means, play the old favorites, but mix them up with new discoveries so that the club patrons can learn new songs to request over and over.)

Along with the seemingly never-ending old vs. new music DJ quandary, there are the always-amusing scuffles that start when the DJ plays things to amuse him or herself. As the Lady of the Manners alluded at the beginning of the chapter, there are many DJs who love to throw an oddball pop hit into the mix to see if anyone will dance to it. On the whole, most club patrons are just as amused as the DJs by these sorts of hijinks and will gleefully lurch onto the dance floor to try to Goth-dance to "Wake Me Up Before You Go-Go" before dissolving into hilarity. But the DJs need to remember that there will always be a few people who are not amused at all by this sort of thing, who will complain endlessly, saying things like, "Ohmygod, they're not even playing Goth music! They're ruining the club! I can't believe people are out there dancing to this crap," and so on. Please try not to laugh directly at these people. The Lady of the Manners agrees they're overreacting and really do need to develop a sense of humor about the Goth scene, but mocking them to their faces is unkind. And to the people fuming that the sanctity of their musical church has been ruined (to use a phrase the Lady of the Manners did indeed once see in reference to this sort of thing), the Lady of the Manners would like to point out that nowhere in the Goth handbook (which doesn't actually exist) does it say that they must listen only to Goth music. Nor does it say that Goth clubs must play only Goth music. But if the Goth handbook did exist, it would probably have quite a few chapters about the absolute necessity of maintaining a sense of humor and how taking oneself dead seriously is, perhaps, a bit ridiculous. But such a Goth handbook doesn't exist, so these poor humorless gothlings will just have to resign themselves to sitting in a darkened corner of the club and seething not-so-quietly to themselves as everyone else runs out to the dance floor to flail around to "I Kissed a Girl."

Why yelling "Freebird" isn't as amusing as you might think and other advice for concertgoers

Concerts are special events. They offer rare chances to see favorite musicians perform live and hear familiar songs in new arrangements. People attending should be respectful and appreciative. Respectful and appreciative does not mean shouting things out at the performers. No questions, no "I love you!" (until the end of the performance, when it's a bit more acceptable to shout praise). Unless, of course, it's a rock concert of some sort, because shrieking one's lungs out is the proper thing to do at those sorts of shows. Oh, and no requests! Because while there may be a song you're longing to hear performed, the band has these things called set lists. Set lists are lists (imagine that) of the songs in the order the band plans to perform them. Many bands only rehearse a certain group of songs for their live act—the ones they think best showcase their talents in a live setting, the songs they know are audience favorites, and sometimes ones they themselves are fond of. Perhaps your favorite song doesn't fall into any of those categories. That doesn't mean you get to shout a request at the band. It is the height of rudeness to do so; it's rude to the band, and it's rude to the rest of the audience. Oh, and it's even ruder to shout requests for songs by other bands. Shouting "Freebird!" in the middle of a concert is tacky and dumb, not funny or ironic.

Another of the Lady of the Manners's pet peeves of concert attendance is the seemingly ever-present talking people. Do not talk through a performance. Even if you aren't interested in what is currently being performed, others around you are. If it is vitally important that you say something to someone, whisper in his or her ear as quietly as you can or leave the auditorium. Oh, and turn off your dratted cell phones. (Again, these bits of advice don't exactly apply to loud rock shows.)

Rules regarding standing, dancing, and moshing at concerts all depend on the types of venues and attendees. If the concert

takes place at a proper sort of theatre with reserved seats, you should stick to your place. Standing up only blocks the view of the people behind you and causes them to be distracted from the concert, get mad, and think longingly of lopping your head off. "But wait!" the Lady of the Manners can here some of you muttering. "What happens if the person in front of me stands up? Aren't I allowed to stand up then?"

No. You aren't. You are only allowed to stand up during a concert if everyone jumps to his or her feet simultaneously, like a herd of lemmings. If it is just a case of one person in front of you standing up, politely get his attention (tapping on the back = good; kicking = bad) and ask him to sit down. If he refuses, tell him you *will* go get an usher and then do so. The Lady of the Manners is all for being swept away by the musical experience but doesn't think that's an excuse for disrupting others' enjoyment.

If the concert is taking place at a club or arena, that's a different story. Seating at those sorts of venues tends to be a free-for-all. It's perfectly acceptable to stand up, but try to make sure you're not standing in front of someone who is seated or who is vastly shorter than you. Those sorts of venues also are perfect for dancing during the show. In fact, many musicians prefer to see people dance and be enthusiastic during a performance, so go right ahead.

As for moshing—well, first of all, is it the sort of music that a person *would* mosh to? If so, you can start thrashing about. But! Don't try to forcibly include people in the moshing, and even in the midst of it, try to not hit people with your flailing arms and legs. Inadvertently punching other concertgoers is rude. (So is deliberately punching other concertgoers, but the Lady of the Manners is assuming you knew that.) If someone near you falls down, help her back up. And for goodness' sake, don't try to shove your way toward the stage. The people who have the coveted spots directly in front of the band are there because they were willing to get to the venue early and wait a ridiculously long time in line. Just because you are able to shove them out of the way doesn't mean that you should.

A Special Section about dealing with or being a tourist at a Goth club or event

No, the Lady of the Manners does not mean the type of tourist who visits other cities and historical landmarks; she means the people who aren't Goths (and have no interest in ever being Goths), who go to Goth clubs, a hotly debated topic in the Goth subculture.

Why is this a topic of never-ending discussion in the Goth world? Well, because opinions about scene tourists are pretty sharply divided. More people in the clubs means that the clubs are making money and Gothic club nights will flourish, not to mention that many clubgoers feel that strict dress codes and "scene-only" door policies are ever-so-slightly on the bad side of elitist. On the other hand, swarms of non-Goths take away from the ambience and atmosphere of a club, and it's more than a little annoying to be treated like a zoo exhibit when you're someplace you visit almost every week.

The Lady of the Manners, while wanting the Goth clubs and event promoters not to starve and to keep hosting fabulous events, is pretty much against tourists. Why? Well . . . many non-gothy types, when they decide to go to the local spooky club, are doing so because they want to feel transgressive or "naughty." "Ooooh, lets go to that place where all those weird and freaky vampire people are!" For them, going to a Goth club has a lot in common with going to an amusement park: zanily dressed characters and the thrill of flirting with what looks dangerous but really isn't. Your Gothic Charm School headmistress has issues with this because she doesn't like the idea of something dear to her (and thousands of other Goths across the world) being turned into a cheap thrill for people who aren't sure how to find their own excitement or entertainment.

Which leads right to the Lady of the Manners's other problem with a lot of club tourists: the whole sexy death chicks nonsense. For whatever reason, a lot of non-Goths assume that Goths are . . . oh dear, how to put this . . . not only sexually deviant, but rather free and indiscriminate in who they practice those behaviors with. These non-Goths seem to believe that people wearing all black, corsets, lace, fishnet, or PVC at a club are not only willing and available but welcome complete strangers walking up and touching them. Which, of course, is not the slightest bit true, but is one of those pervasive misunderstandings about the Gothic subculture.

Now, if you're a non-Goth and have patiently read this far, the Lady of the Manners does indeed have some advice for you, advice that isn't, "Don't ever even think of going to a Goth club."

Thing the First: As the Lady of the Manners has said previously, examine your motives for wanting to check out the local gothy haunts. Seeing friends, wanting to learn more about the local Goth scene, wanting to hear more of that Goth music you like—those are all good reasons. Even going because you feel like spending an evening at a club watching Goths in all their spooky finery is a perfectly acceptable reason. But going to deliberately antagonize or harass people, or to get smashed and slur out bad pick-up lines at the other club-goers because "everyone knows" that Goths are sluts? Those are *bad* reasons to go to a Goth club, and if those are what motivate you to attend the local spooky club, do everyone (including yourself) a favor and stay home.

Thing the Second: If you want to dance, dance. Really, that's what the dance floor is there for. However (and you knew the Lady of the Manners would have a "however," didn't you?), be aware that dancing at a Goth club is slightly different from dancing at other nightspots. For one thing, most Goths don't dance *with* anyone else. So don't worry about finding someone to dance with. That also means not, er, aggressively dancing *at* someone else or grabbing him or her to demonstrate your dirty dancing prowess. (Cast your mind back to Chapter 2: Remember what the Lady of the Manners said about not touching someone without getting permission first? That holds true for dance floor antics too.) Do not attempt to start a mosh pit, do not slam into other dancers, and do not wave your drink around in the air.

Thing the Third: Speaking of drinks, you do realize that if you are in a new-to-you social environment, you should probably avoid excessive drinking, don't you? Navigating a new club or social scene can be tricky enough without blurring your perceptions. Not to mention that you don't want the first impressions people have of you to be that you're some sort of stumbling, drunken boor.

Thing the Fourth: For goodness' sake, don't just lurk there in a darkened corner, sipping your drink. Go talk to people! If you're there with friends, have them introduce you to other people at the club. If you're there by yourself, at least introduce yourself to some people. No, the regular denizens of the club probably won't greet you with outpourings of glee and wide-open arms, but at least make the effort to talk to people. What should you talk to them about? You could compliment them on their outfits or dancing. You could ask them if this is a typical night at the club and mention that you haven't been to many gothy clubs. But, the Lady of the Manners must warn you, do your very best to avoid sounding like you're trying out your collection of pick-up lines. Yes, even if the creature of darkness you're chatting with is devastatingly gorgeous and you would like to ask her out. Goths have a not-unreasonable distaste for clubland tourists saying things like "So d'ya come here often?" to them. Many Goths consider "their" club to be just that—theirs—and understandably get a wee bit upset when tourists behave like ye olde spooky club is nothing but a meat market.

TEN

Where Do We Go from Here?

The possible Future of Goth and the Lady of the Manners's hopes for it (plus a couple of her fears, though she's sure they won't come to pass)

The Future of Goth. That has a nicely portentous ring to it, doesn't it? As if it should be a page in a dusty book, protected through the ages by a secret society of black-clad decadents . . .

No, the Lady of the Manners hasn't taken leave of her senses; nor does she believe she's part of an ancient secret society. (She keeps telling you that there is no Secret Goth Cabal for a reason, Snarklings, and it's not to hide in plain sight.)

Anyway, the future of Goth. From the Lady of the Manners's viewpoint (languishing gracefully on a fainting couch, possibly with a cup of tea in hand), the Gothic subculture will not only

continue to thrive but grow even larger than it currently is. In many ways, the Gothic subculture is a *subculture* in name only. There are now sympathetic Goth characters on mainstream TV shows and in more than just niche horror novels. There are yearly Goth-themed festivals all over the world and Goth-focused panels at large conventions. Every Halloween produces more and more pre-packaged "Goth" costumes for people who want to dabble in our spooky world for an evening. All of these are signs that, no matter how negatively some in the mainstream media try to portray us, more and more people realize that Goths aren't a danger to themselves or others, that we're just people with different interests and aesthetics.

Of course, there are those amongst our spooky extended family who are not at all pleased by this trend of mainstream . . . well, not acceptance, but acknowledgment. They feel that Goth is diluted by it, that the whole concept is losing (if it hasn't already lost) what made it different and special. The Lady of the Manners somewhat understands those complaints (and her understanding grows when she witnesses the new and cheesy Gothic cheerleader costumes that hit the shelves every October) but thinks that perhaps those people are overreacting just the tiniest bit. Yes, it's a bit strange to think that what started out as a shadowy refuge has become well known enough to be regarded as a profitable target demographic, but as the Lady of the Manners has said before, the more "mainstream" awareness of what Goth really is, the fewer young babybats will have to go through the bullying and harassment that many ElderGoths suffered. The more people who have even a vague understanding about Goth, the smaller the chance that Goths will be regarded with suspicion, fear, and hostility. Or so the Lady of the Manners hopes.

So what else about the future of Goth? As the Gothic community expands, there will be more and more splinter groups, groups who have common roots

and some similar interests but don't see themselves as falling under the Gothic subculture's shady parasol. One example is the Steampunk movement: people fascinated by the future that never was. Clockwork mechanisms, airships, sky pirates, adventurers, mad scientists, and resourceful street urchins, all dressed up in Victorian-tinged finery. (Finery that shows the effects of being worn while crawling around giant machines or is smudged with soot and chemicals from the latest mad science experiment but still is not your run-of-the-mill khakis and T-shirts.) The Lady of the Manners has seen Steampunk-themed events held at Goth gatherings and clubs and is quite tickled by the "family resemblance" between shadowy Goths and their sepia-toned Steampunk cousins.

To further muddle the lines between Steampunk and Goth, it seems that a fair number of Steampunkers were once Goths but decided they wanted a change of pace. The Lady of the Manners thinks that such subcultural migration is a very good thing but hopes that people moving away from Goth don't ever refer to their explorations and branching out as "growing out of the whole Goth thing" nor look down their noses at their previous family of black-clad people.

One of the things that fascinates the Lady of the Manners about the Steampunk movement is the extremely strong thread of make-believe or fantasy that seemingly binds the whole community together. While the Goth subculture has a strong fondness for elaborate outfits and decor, the Lady of the Manners can't remember hearing Goths ask whether they needed to come up with a character or persona before playing with fancy clothing. Those very questions, along with asking for help creating an alternate persona, seem to come up with amazing frequency on the various online Steampunk communities the Lady of the Manners watches.

(The answers to such queries seem to be equally divided between people offering help in fleshing out a character and people saying, "Dress how you want! You don't need a separate persona to wear a top hat and goggles, for goodness' sake.")

Another community that is a hybrid flower sharing roots with the Goth family tree is the Gothic Lolita movement. Originating in Japan, Gothic Lolita is a style that aims to create a doll-like silhouette. Knee-length skirts puffed out with petticoats, frilly blouses, and ruffles galore are some of the key themes in Gothic Lolita fashion. While the Gothic side of Gothic Lolita wouldn't look out of place at any Goth gathering, the Gothic Lolita community has a sweeter, more pastel side. Most Goths would widen their black-rimmed eyes in response to the outfits made from fabrics featuring prints of teddy bears, cookies, berries, and other sweet things (which explains why that particular strain of Lolita is called *Sweet* Lolita). The doll-like aesthetic of Gothic Lolita is one that has been seen time and time again in the Goth subculture; true, the Goth version of "doll-like" often brings to mind the sort of unnerving porcelain dolls seen in movies where there's probably a high body count, but those creepy dolls are still, well, dolls. They're just going to a tea party of a much darker type.

In the Lady of the Manners's experience, devotees of Gothic Lolita are a touch uneasy about being associated with the Goth subculture. While the Gothic side of the Gothic Lolita subculture has similar tastes in motifs to Goth (coffins, skulls, bats, veils, a wardrobe that would probably not be out of place at a Victorian-era funeral), many of the Gothic Lolitas wouldn't consider themselves to be Goths because they are not interested in everything that the Goth subculture embraces. Dark and fantastical literature and movies, the music, finding beauty in dark and unexpected places; many of the denizens of Gothic Lolita don't seek out such things but just want to wear fancy clothing and attend picnics and tea parties.

(Let the Lady of the Manners state *right now* that she is completely in favor of people wearing fancy clothing and attending picnics and tea parties, regardless of the subcultural affiliation they claim. The Lady of the Manners firmly believes that the world would be a pleasanter place if more people would try to include more relaxing and frivolous events in their lives.)

In addition to the various subcultures that can be considered fantastical siblings to Goth, the Lady of the Manners suspects that the future of Goth will see a renewed interest in some of the original dark flourishes of the Gothic subculture. It's already happening; the deathrock or batcave strain of Goth is experiencing something of a dark renaissance, with whiteface makeup and shredded fishnets for all. And don't think that the reanimation of deathrock is merely some nostalgia trip; not only are the old-school ghouls lurching out of their crypts (after backcombing and lacquering their mohawks back into an upright position), but new creatures of darkness are learning how to use black and purple eye shadow to contour their gaunt cheeks.

But what about the Lady of the Manners's fears about the future of Goth? Oh, merely that Goth will no longer be a vibrant and ever-changing subculture but will become stagnant and moribund. (*Moribund,* as in becoming obsolete and dying, as opposed to *morbid,* as in being characterized by notions of gloom and decay.) Does the Lady of the Manners think that Goth will stagnate and die off? No. But she does sometimes worry that all the sub-subcultures that splinter off from Goth may be so intent on building their little niches and adding their own "requirements" or qualifications that ridiculous and artificial boundaries will spring up like poisonous mushrooms. Things like "Oh, if you are into [black metal, Steampunk, Gothic Lolita, gothabilly, or other splinter group vaguely associated with Goth], then you aren't a Goth." The Lady of the Manners has railed about labels before, but to sum up her views about them: labels are useful in that they can impart a lot of information about your views and interests, but goodness gracious, don't use them as a template you can never, ever stray from.

Mind you, every subculture has adherents who seem to be poised to proclaim, "Goth [or Steampunk, metal, emo, punk, etc.] is dead!" every chance they can find. The people making these sorts of statements are, in the Lady of the Manners's eyes, a very necessary part of every subculture. Not because they're right in their declarations of doom and "The scene is dead!" (to quote the band Rasputina, "The scene isn't what it used to be / The scene is never what it used to be"), but because declarations that a certain subculture is dead are, strangely enough, a sign of growth and change. It's not that Goth (or deathrock, or Steampunk, and so on) is dead; it's that the subculture has branched out from what the naysayers are familiar or comfortable with. Also, it indicated that the subculture has grown enough that it is no longer a teeny-tiny niche that only a certain few "cooler-than-you" types are aware of. (The Lady of the Manners is sure that you know the type of people she's referring to, Snarklings: people who feel the need to abandon anything when it becomes even slightly popular with more than five people on a secret Internet forum, people who apparently have made it their life's goal to roll their eyes and sneer dismissively at anything anyone else likes. The Lady of the Manners feels a bit sorry for them and occasionally wonders if they ever get tired of expending so much effort to be so *very* avant-garde and fashion-forward.)

Of course, there's also the concern that the Goth subculture will shift and change so much that it will become almost unrecognizable to some members of the community. This already happened on a much smaller scale when it seemed like cybergoth and tweedly-beep-oontz-oontz ebm music became the dominant genres at many Goth clubs. Now the Lady of the Manners realizes that her perceptions may be a trifle influenced by the fact that the cybergoth style and ebm music are very much *not* her cup of tea. But for a while it seemed like the subculture was becoming about thumpy synthpop music and outfits made from stretchy fabric with UV-reactive trim, and clots of velvet

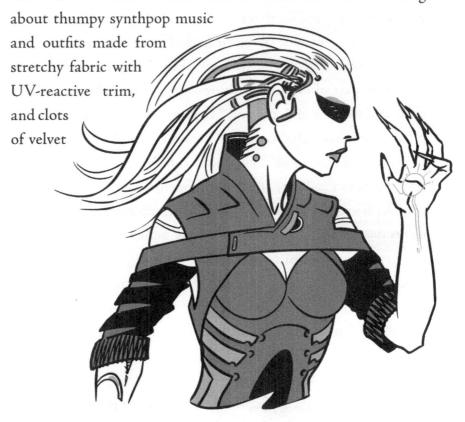

and lace-clad people had to wait patiently (or not so patiently) to hear a song that featured guitars. But the tastes of the subculture went through another tidal shift, and nowadays it seems there are equal numbers of cybergoths and traditional Goths, with a sprinkling of vampires, steampunks, and deathrockers everywhere.

One of the other fears about the future of Goth that sometimes scampers through the Lady of the Manners's mind is that Goth really will, for the most part, turn into a phase that people "grow out of." That more and more youngsters will spend a little time dabbling in the shadow-draped subculture and then feel that they *must* leave such things behind in order to move into the adult world. That eventually, the only Goths over the age of sixteen will be a tiny minority that constantly has to try and explain that Goth is not synonymous with teenage angst. Again, the Lady of the Manners doesn't really feel this situation will come to pass; the numbers of grown-up Goths who see no reason to give up their dark and gloom-shrouded ways and are successful in their chosen paths and professions are constantly growing. As more Goths refuse to "grow out of" what is presumed by the uninformed to be a juvenile fascination with the darker, more otherworldly aspects of life, perhaps the future will hold less harassment and bullying for everyone, not just the strange and black-clad types.

"But what about the Lady of the Manners's *hopes* for the future of Goth?" you may be asking. Oh, that's an easy question, Snarklings. The Lady of the Manners hopes that Goth gains more understanding and acceptance in the mainstream. Enough acceptance that people realize showing a preference for sumptuous black clothing, dramatic makeup, and wanting to hold a picnic in a graveyard are not signs of a dangerous and deranged mind. Enough understanding of what Goth is and where it comes from, so that when the mainstream media or fashion industry decide to dip their collective toes into our dark waters, they don't feel the need to plaster everything with disclaimers about how *their* current version of Goth-influenced whatever is "Goth, but elegant" or isn't about "angsty teens."

The Lady of the Manners also hopes that the Goth subculture keeps growing, keeps coming up with new and fascinating interpretations of the idea of dark glamour and otherworldliness. That all the fledgling babybats or gothlings who realize they feel at home in the Goth world are accepted for who they are and who they *want* to become.

In the end, it all comes down to the Lady of the Manners's fervent hopes that Goths and non-Goths will no longer view each other with suspicion or raised eyebrows, and that the Goth subculture will always be around, no matter what the future holds for everyone.